FORC[ED TO]
MARRY HIM

A Lifetime of Tradition and the Will to Break It

DAVINDER
KAUR

Forced to Marry Him
A Lifetime of Tradition and the Will to Break It
Text copyright © 2021 Davinder Kaur

All Rights Reserved in accordance with the U.S. Copyright Act of 1976, the scanning, uploading, and electronic sharing of any part of this book without the permission of the publisher or author constitute unlawful piracy and theft of the author's intellectual property. If you would like to use material from this book (other than for review purposes), prior written permission must be obtained by contacting the publisher at davinderkaur@me.com. Thank you for your support of author's rights.

Although the author has made every effort to ensure that the information in this book was correct at publication, the author does not assume and hereby disclaims liability to any party for loss, damage, or disruption caused by errors or omissions, whether such errors or omissions result from negligence, accident, or any other cause.

This book is not intended as a substitute for the medical advice of physicians or therapist. The reader should regularly consult a physician or therapist in matters relating to his/her health, and particularly with respect to any symptoms that may require diagnosis or medical attention.

Published in the United States of America.
Cover designer: LeTeisha Newton — Beyond DEF
Editor: Tiffany Fox & C.A. Houghton — Beyond DEF
Interior Layout & eBook Adaptation: Deena Rae — EBook Builders

File version: 202110025.009

Contents

Forced to Marry Him .... e
Dedication .... g
Acknowledgments i
Introduction 1
Preface 3
Childhood 7
Family 11
Family Secrets 25
The Shop in Bradford 27
Community 33
School 35
The Culture and Tradition 37
The Picture 43
The Engagement 47
Writing and Calling 51
1985 Trip to India 55
The Move to Hull 63
The Youth Training Scheme 69
Developing My Own Independence 71
The Escape 75
Arrival in London 77

The Phone Call Home 85
The Return to Hull..89
Hello, Denmark! 95
Forced Marriage Day...101
The "Honeymoon" 107
Return to Denmark and Our New Place 113
The Control Freak..119
My Dad's Arrival and the Unforgivable Incident 123
The Second Escape 129
Return to the Apartment...133
Freedom at Last..137
Two More Forced Marriages in the Family 141
The Trip to Germany..145
The Trip to Australia..147
Hello, America 151
Family Dynamics and My Life Now..153
Telling My Story for The First Time 159
Discovering Others Like Me and My Path to Activism 163
Why Forced Marriages and Child Marriages Have to be Illegal ..169
Subsequent Speaking Events...171
Conclusion 175
How to Find Out More..179
About the Author..181

Forced to Marry Him

In the late 1980s, Davinder Kaur was forced to marry a man she didn't know. When she was only fourteen years old, the marriage was arranged and set to occur when she turned eighteen. After four long years of internal turmoil and despair, she had two choices: adhere to the customs and traditions of her family or risk bringing dishonor to their home. Davinder didn't like either option, so she made a plan—a plan to survive.

In *Forced to Marry Him: A Lifetime of Tradition and the Will to Break It*, Kaur tells of the pain, lies, and betrayal she suffered at the hands of those who were meant to protect her the most. But her story doesn't end there. Davinder's willingness to speak out and fight not only saved her life but the lives of many other women and young girls over the years. She offers courage and strength to those who can't advocate for themselves, and she works with organizations all over the world to help end arranged and forced marriages. Kaur gives a voice to the voiceless as she breaks down walls to eradicate cultural and traditional abuse.

Dedication

To my children, Nikita, Luca, and Chandra, you mean the world to me, and I am so very proud of you all. Thanks for putting up with me.

To my mum, I hope one day you will understand. I love you and have forgiven you.

To Jasvinder Sanghera and Fraidy Reiss, you have inspired me so much with your courage, determination, and passion to help victims of child marriage, forced marriage, and honor abuse. You have saved countless lives and have made a difference to so many. You have created change. I salute you.

H

Acknowledgments

I'd like to express special thanks to everyone who was there for me along my journey. I appreciate my Burger King co-workers and anyone else who stood up for me. I'm thankful for all who believed in me, encouraged me to tell my story, and reminded me I was doing the right thing. Your support means everything to me.

There are numerous organizations that support victims of honor-based abuse, child marriage, and forced marriage. Thank you for what you do. You are instrumental in serving a vitally important purpose.

Introduction

When I was growing up in Bradford in northern England, I had the same dreams most young girls have. I read Mills and Boon books—romance stories—and dreamed of experiencing a great romance before marriage. That's how I thought things were meant to be. After all, life and love were portrayed that way in my books and on television shows I'd seen. I had witnessed the engagement of Princess Diana and Prince Charles on television and in the newspapers when I was about thirteen years old, and what a fairytale romance that was, even though it ended sadly and tragically for Princess Diana.

I viewed these occurrences and wanted them for myself as I grew up in a westernized society. Little did I know, I would not be allowed these dreams because my parents, who had immigrated to England from India when they were very young, were expected to carry on Indian traditions and culture. They did not want their daughters or son to engage in romances. Instead, they would arrange marriages for each of us. This reality was the opposite of the ideals we were growing up with. We were raised in westernized society but were expected to keep easternized values. That wasn't an easy thing to do.

Now that I am older, I recognize I grew up with abusive gaslighting. I wasn't aware of the manipulation at the time, nor was I aware there was even a term for what I experienced. Gaslighting is a psychological manipulation in which the abuser sows seeds of doubt into a person's experience to the point they question their own reality. It really is a pernicious thing to do to someone.

Not only was my childhood taken from me, but my dreams and ambitions were stripped away as well. My freedom was snatched, and what's worse, I experienced atrocities in which my own family was complicit.

My story is painful, but I believe it's important to share it. If even *one* person is saved, it is worth every word. It feels good to know it might make a difference.

Preface

Warning: I was in a dark place when I was young. This preface contains a very brief mention of suicide. I felt it was important to convey how my circumstances affected my mental health, pushing me to drastic measures. If this is a trigger for you, please skip to the first chapter.

When I was eleven or twelve, I didn't think life was worth living anymore. I had decided to slash my neck and had chosen the instrument carefully. The knife was perfect for chopping onions, so I figured it should be good enough to do what I needed to accomplish. Standing in the kitchen, I held it to my skin and exerted pressure, hoping the blade would penetrate my flesh and cause enough harm to end my pain and suffering. The tip of the knife was cold against my skin, but it didn't pierce the soft tissue. I then tried to chop my neck like I would the onions, going from left to right in a straight line, but nothing happened.

Will they even care?
Will they cry?

I doubted it. They probably would just curse me, especially my mother.

"Stupid, idiotic girl! How could she do this? Why did she do this?"

My mother asked all these questions and more, acting as if she had no clue why I had taken my life, but if she really dug deep, would *she* even have the self-awareness to know her actions had caused my death?

Thankfully, I was not successful. I lacked the strength and courage to carry through with my plan, and I also had no clue what I was doing. I didn't apply enough pressure to the instrument to force it into my skin or do any real harm. I don't think I had the power or the will, as I obviously didn't try hard enough. One thing was certain: I'd had enough of being put down. I felt I wasn't loved or wanted. Nothing I did was ever good enough; I was criticized continuously, and I felt my life wasn't fair or that I wasn't needed.

I stared at the knife in my hands for a long time before I cleaned it. It would be like washing away the attempt—nobody would know anything, and the knife could be used for its proper purpose again. I slid the sponge over the shiny silver blade, drenching it with liquid and scrubbing it thoroughly, even rubbing the sponge over the wooden handle. Over the years, I thought I had done some damage because I noticed the shadow of a line across my neck. I thought I had somehow caused it, but now I realize it couldn't have been the knife. I would have bled.

I was not told ending one's life is wrong, but I was exposed to this way of thinking from a very young age. I can't recall if I learned this from television or from conversations I overheard. You may ask, "Is it cultural or spiritual?" I can honestly say these belief systems were more likely from the western culture I was exposed to versus the Indian culture of my family.

I am ashamed to admit I attempted to take my life. Nobody should have enough power over me to cause me to do something so drastic and dangerous like that. I have never spoken to anyone about what I tried to do; this is the first time I have disclosed this secret. There is absolutely no reason I would or should ever want to end my life. I believe things will get better, no matter how bad they seem.

My life is a precious gift, and I am thankful to be alive so I can share my story. My journey began in northern England in what could be characterized as an unhappy childhood. I was not allowed to have freedom or choice, and I had no voice. I would gradually realize life wasn't fair, and it wasn't like it was in the books.

Childhood

I was born in Bradford about fifty years ago, give or take a few years. Bradford is a dull city. All the houses were made of black or gray bricks. Occasionally, there were some bright-colored doors—pink, green, yellow, and so forth—but the colors didn't compensate for all those dark, drab buildings. The weather was also dreary, as I don't recall any sunny days, although I'm sure there must have been some.

Bradford was an industrial city near Leeds and Manchester. It had many factories and textile mills. Most of the residents worked in the mills, weaving wool or cotton. My grandma, my mum, and two of my aunties all worked in the same mill. One of the aunties was my mum's sister and the other was her sister-in-law—I called her *Mami Ji* (this is the Punjabi name given to your mum's brother's wife). It was the type of job one inherited, and I could have ended up working in the same factory if we had stayed in Bradford or hadn't opened our shops.

Bradford could very easily be called the "Second India." We had a mixed neighborhood consisting of Indians, Pakistanis, and English neighbors.

We spoke Punjabi really well until we started school. Our teachers discouraged us from speaking it and encouraged us to speak only English.

My kindergarten teacher made an announcement on my first day. "Make sure to tell your parents you should only speak English at home. It will really help you if that's all you speak. You really have to make an effort. If you listen to what I'm suggesting, you're going to be better off."

Our parents weren't happy, but they complied. We mostly spoke English from that point on, with my grandma being the exception. The more we spoke English, the more self-conscious we became about our Punjabi. I have the same feeling about my Punjabi today. My brother and sisters have gotten better at it because they stayed in England and are surrounded by Punjabi speakers.

My mum was a pretty woman. She was quite fashionable, did her hair nicely, and wore bangles, makeup, and beautiful clothes. I was extremely proud when she came to our elementary school to pick me up or attend any plays, as I always thought she looked better than the other mothers. My mum wasn't very tall. I took after her in appearance and height and have been told we look identical. She didn't have very dark skin but rather had the lighter complexion of the people from northern India—the Punjab. Mum knew English well because she had moved to England when she was nine years old.

My father was taller than her, and they were about the same age. He and his family had moved to England from the Punjab when he was approximately ten. My dad had naturally curly hair and darker skin than my mum. He smoked a lot and drank alcohol quite a bit too. He was out all night and didn't return home on many occasions. I felt sorry for Mum. She tried leaving him once or twice, and she threw him out or told him not to come back, but he always did. I can't say their marriage was happy; I remember the yelling and the lack of joy.

"You just come home to eat and fill your tummy. After you eat, you sleep, and then you go out and drink again. I've had enough of it," she yelled in Punjabi. They always spoke to each other in their native tongue.

My dad was more of the silent type and almost never disciplined us. Mum took care of making sure we stayed in tight control. She ruled our household and, to me, appeared to be a strong woman who was unafraid to speak up and say what was on her mind. I've heard of many Indian women who are very timid and scared of their husbands. They quietly do their work and will not verbalize their thoughts and feelings to their spouse. Not my mum!

"I don't see why I should be doing your washing for you. You don't deserve it. You don't pull your weight in this house. I'm left doing all the work in the shop and the housework. You just come home to eat, and we do all the work. Then you go and gamble away all the money! Just get out!" she screamed.

"Come on, Preeto, you know it's not quite like that," he replied, trying to placate her and calm her down, even reaching for her arm in a gesture of peace as he sought forgiveness in his own way. He liked referring to her by her nickname, which was short for Jaspreet.

My mum pulled away, not wanting him to come anywhere near her during these times. One stern look from her could make someone dread they had done something wrong and were in deep trouble. My dad knew better than to press his luck.

"Stay away from me," she warned in a stone-cold tone that could freeze a person on the spot. "How much did you gamble this time? You don't think about anyone else but yourself. You ought to have some shame. You have a family you are responsible for, but you run from everything and throw your money away. Why don't you just give it to me instead?"

"Preeto, I didn't spend too much. I just passed some time," he mumbled, as though this was a good excuse.

My dad gambled, smoked, drank, and I don't believe he was entirely faithful either. He did all the things a woman didn't want her man to do. Mum practically brought us up on her own. When he came home, we had to arrange his dinner quickly and give it to him, no matter what time it was.

My dad wanted Indian food all the time, and there had to be at least one meat dish, usually a chicken or lamb curry. Mum was vegetarian, so there had to be one Indian dish without meat. But my brother always preferred English food: chips (the thicker version of fries here in the United States) with fish fingers, or chips with sausages, or chips with just about anything, plus peas or beans on the side.

Dad was a bus driver and looked after us in the evening quite often because Mum worked late hours at the textile mill. He was quite good at making sardine curry and egg curry. He made *rotis*, also known as *chupattis*—a type of bread that is rolled out and placed on a griddle called a *tava*. His *rotis* were large and not very round, and we sometimes laughed about that. He chopped onions and added garlic, ginger, chili peppers, tomatoes, and spices. This preparation is called a *torka* and is in just about every Indian dish. The main ingredient—chicken, lamb, vegetables, or eggs—was added at the very end.

My dad made warm milk with Ovaltine for us just before we went to bed. The malt powder added a soothing quality believed to help make you sleepy. Sometimes, we just had a cup of milk and a biscuit. It was nice when Dad looked after us as we enjoyed his misshapen *rotis* and the more relaxed evenings.

Family

My brother, Mandeep, is a year older than me, and I have two sisters. Kuljeet is a year and a half younger, and Sabina is seven years younger. Kuljeet and I used to fight over dolls. She broke mine, and then I did the same to her dolls. We used to dress like twins, even though there was more than a year between us. It was easier for my mum to buy two of the same outfits. A lot of kids at school constantly asked us if we were twins.

When Sabina was brought home as a newborn from the hospital, I did little tasks such as warming up the formula and fetching things for Mum. Later, when I was older, I helped get her ready in the morning. I combed her hair and braided it or tied it up in ponytails.

Mandeep was very self-assured. My family paid the most attention to him. Being the first-born *and* a boy was important. It meant a lot to my mum and dad and all our relatives. Most Indians value having boys instead of girls. Boys are considered "worthy" and are to be respected and treated differently. To some degree, Mandeep was treated like a prince. My sisters and I were required to make the food he wanted, retrieve his cups of tea whenever he demanded them, wash his clothes, clean his room, and so much more.

Girls, according to general Indian thinking, are only good for housework and marriage. We not only have to pay the utmost respect to our parents but to our brothers as well. I got along well with my siblings, but I have always felt I wasn't good enough. This feeling was mostly instilled in me by my mum. I felt she bullied me. I believed I couldn't do enough to improve her impression of me and make her see I could be just as good as my brother and sisters.

Mandeep was the loudest compared to the rest of us and was able to get away with almost anything—even if it was bad—because he was a boy. He used to call me *moti,* meaning "fat," because I was a little chubby back then. My sisters echoed the name calling, but I knew they were all joking; I didn't take it personally.

One day, a boy from school was walking home in front of me. He somehow knew I was behind him and, for no apparent reason, turned around and kicked me several times and punched me in the stomach. I received several scratches from him too. I was very hurt and bewildered and cried all the way home. Mandeep found out who the boy was and taught him a lesson that night or the next day. My brother gave him a good beating, and the boy never picked on me again. Mandeep looked out for me and protected me. I've always respected him for that.

We were a traditional Punjabi family. Many Punjabi families in Bradford went to the temple, practiced their faith, and followed their culture and traditions. This involved wearing Punjabi clothing to the Sikh temple and for special occasions such as parties and weddings. However, we weren't devout Sikhs. They were very religious, avoided eating meat, and covered their heads. Sikh men wear turbans, and Sikh women wear a scarf called a *chunni*. My dad and brother didn't wear turbans, and we didn't cover our heads or wear Punjabi outfits all the time. Devout Sikhs also avoid drinking or smoking. As a non-devout Punjabi family, we ate meat but abided by our religion to the degree that we didn't eat beef because cows are considered sacred.

Mum made a lot of the decisions in our household. When we wanted to go on field trips or trips abroad for school, she told us she had to check with our dad.

"Your dad said no to the field trip. It's too expensive, and it's really not necessary for you to go."

"Please, Mum. Can I please go?" my sister or I pleaded.

"No, what did I just say? Why do I have to tell you more than once? You need to learn to listen. The answer is no." There was to be no further discussion.

I thought this was incredibly unfair. Mandeep was allowed to go on a field trip with school, and he went to France on a separate occasion. Money didn't seem to be a factor then; it was only an obstacle when it came to my sister and me.

Boys had much more leniency and freedom. They could go to college and receive further education, but the girls were held back. Boys could play outside and hang out with their friends, but girls weren't supposed to be out of their parents' sight. It was almost as though we were bound get into trouble if we were allowed to be somewhere independent of them.

Dad was more relaxed about how we did things in the home, and he rarely told us what to do. On the other hand, Mum liked to see everything done just the way she preferred. If it wasn't, she gave us a hard stare and scowled, contorting her face into angry or annoyed expressions. She almost always raised her hand, ready to slap. This let us know what would happen if we didn't comply with her wishes. She often carried out her open threat. We felt the sharp pain of her hand across our faces or the back of our heads many times.

"Ow! That *hurt*! Stop! Please, stop," we cried. "Please, stop. Please, don't do it again!"

"You kids are the absolute worst! How many times have I told you not to do it that way or to do it the way I've shown you so many times! When is it going to get into your head?" she yelled. "You know I have really high blood pressure, and you are making it worse! Don't you know better than to aggravate me?"

Her constant gaslighting made us more afraid of upsetting her, but we didn't know what it was back then. We feared being the cause of her high blood pressure, and the yelling and blaming made us more afraid of her. We were overcome with guilt because she made us believe *we* were the reason she was continuously agitated. But she was our mum, and we didn't want anything to happen to her because we loved her.

My sisters and I weren't allowed much freedom, and everything was controlled to a large degree. If the dishes weren't picked up from the table promptly after a meal, my mum yelled.

"Do you really want me to go and take the dishes?"

"Don't you see that the dishes need taking away?"

If we left dishes in the sink overnight, we felt her wrath.

"How many times do you need to be told that you are not supposed to leave anything in the sink?"

"Everything has to be washed and put away. Why do I have to keep telling you time and time again?"

We were scared when she was mad, and we rushed to take care of it because we feared her hard slap.

When we were young and lived in our first house on Paley Road, we were put in the cellar on several occasions. We were terrified of the mice down there. We heard them scuttling around as soon as my mum dragged us through the cellar door and switched off the light while we were still on the stairs. It was pitch-black with the lights off, making it even more frightening. We were afraid the mice would clamber over our slipper-clad feet. The cellar smelled of spices and dampness. We had the choice to stay on the stairs or walk downstairs into the actual cellar, but we avoided going down the stairs as much as possible. The light switch wasn't accessible from the cellar side of the door; it was on the other side. As much as we didn't want to go down all the way, we didn't have much of a choice if we wanted to get to the switch at the bottom so we had *some* light.

The space was huge and set up like another kitchen, but it was bigger than the one upstairs. Once the light was on, we saw an occasional mouse scuttling across the corner of the room or even up the wall. I am terrified of mice to this day, and I owe a lot of my fear to being locked up with them in the cellar in Bradford.

As frightened as we were of the space, it was great for cooking curries because the smells were contained downstairs. A dining table and a few comfortable chairs were placed in front of the large wood-burning fireplace.

I cried and pleaded to be released from the cellar. "Sorry. Please let me come back up. I won't do it again!"

Constantly apologizing for small things, such as not putting away the dishes, is a response to gaslighting. This happens when the victim believes or is manipulated to behave in an expected way to appease the abuser.

Mum was ruthless in her punishment and screamed from the other side of the door, "I'll teach you a lesson to never do that again, you bad girl!"

We were mostly punished for not answering her the way she wanted us to. For example, she found it unacceptable if she asked us to do something for her and we said we couldn't do the task right away. Mum wanted immediate obedience a hundred percent of the time and no excuses. She was to be treated like the Queen who couldn't be denied her wishes, and we had to be the obedient servants.

We led a very sheltered life. I remember being allowed to play outside up until I was nearly nine years old. I don't recall playing outside much more after that. I think this had something to do with me getting older. I had to learn how to behave in a more mature and responsible way.

I started helping with household tasks when I was seven. As I grew older, I became more involved with routine chores. We washed the dishes by hand—we didn't have dishwashers back then—and we dried them with a towel called a "tea-towel" before putting everything away. I typically washed the dishes while my sister, Kuljeet, dried them. Sometimes, it was the other way around. We cleared the tables and helped serve the guests. My brother rode his bike or played outside with his friends while my sister and I did the chores.

My mum wasn't happy with my efforts, no matter how much I worked.

"You're too slow; why are you so slow?"

"Your sister is so much faster than you. Why can't you learn to be faster? It's not good to be so slow. You have to be faster."

I felt constantly attacked and, again, recognize this as gaslighting. I was always compared to Kuljeet. I did most of the cooking while she mostly did the cleaning, but I cleaned a lot too. I recall constantly cleaning the bathroom and kitchen. I also washed clothes by hand because we didn't have a washer or dryer.

I preferred cooking more than cleaning, as I felt I wasn't criticized as much with my cooking attempts. I spent hours scrubbing and cleaning the bathtub and shower stall, but Mum always criticized my efforts by taking me back to the bathroom to declare her dissatisfaction.

"Do you call this cleaning? What's this? Do you see the hair you left here, and do you see that grime over there in the corner? You're not done. Go do it again!"

"Okay, Mum." I was frustrated that I had to spend more time cleaning, and I wondered how I could have missed it the first time. "I will clean it again. Sorry." I always had to say sorry.

I learned to cook at a young age by watching my mother make things time and time again. I started to make *atta,* the dough for *chupattis,* when I was eight or nine. I helped prepare curries. I cut onions and chopped ginger, garlic, and chilis many times. I learned to shred fresh coriander by finely chopping it and then used it to garnish the curries.

I ironed all our clothes, even the underwear, towels, and sheets. This was such a tedious job. I used to open the ironing table and spend an hour or two ironing in front of the television. Next, I had to put away all the clothes. These tasks had to be completed every week.

Kuljeet and I argued about how I did more work than she did. She always disagreed and said she did more than me. One day, I had to let my sister wash the dishes because my mum made fun of me in front of my grandma. She called me names, such as *bamari,* which meant "poorly" or "not well." It was her way of saying I was slow at everything because there was something wrong with me.

"Look at the *bamari.* I don't know what is wrong with her. Why can't she speed up?" she asked my grandma before returning her attention to me. "We don't have all day for you to take your time with the dishes!"

My grandma nodded and laughed but didn't say anything to support me. Sometimes, she stayed quiet.

"I'm not a *bamari*." Not knowing if I would get in trouble for sticking up for myself or not, I still tried to defend myself.

"You're not a *bamari*? Really? Then why are you so slow? What's wrong with you?" Mum asked again, insinuating in a very manipulative way that something was seriously wrong with me. This was another example of gaslighting, but I had no clue what it was at the time.

The next day, I made a point of getting to the dishes first and working really fast, pointing out that I had done the dishes faster than Kuljeet, but they shrugged it off. My sister took her cue from our mum and denied my declarations or stated I hadn't done something properly.

She pointed at a smear I'd left on a glass. "Look at how you washed this. Do you call this washing?"

They never gave me any recognition or benefit of the doubt. I sometimes felt as if they ganged up on me, that no one was ever on my side. My sister enjoyed showing she was better at everything.

"You're too slow and need to be like me," she teased. It didn't hurt as much when it came from my sister.

"Wash that again, and make sure you are washing the dishes properly," Mum interjected, making it clear she was upset with me and not proud that I had somehow been faster. Mum's words were hurtful and didn't boost my confidence.

Whenever I return to England to visit my family, I feel inferior when I enter the kitchen. I am still subjected to comments such as "You're so slow" or "Oh, you helped out?" and then snide laughter from my mum and sister-in-law. They praise my sister, but I still can't do enough to satisfy them. Sometimes, I don't want to bother with helping, but then I hear whispering and bitter comments such as "She just sat there and didn't help." My family hasn't changed much over the years, and no one should have to get used to that.

When I was young, I often had to walk to the corner store and buy necessities for the household. They consisted of things like food, paper products, odds and ends, and my mum's feminine products. I didn't know what the sanitary items were for because we didn't speak about "uncomfortable" issues in my family.

Mum never talked about relationships or our bodies and the changes we would go through as we grew older. When I first started my menstrual cycle at age ten, I was horrified and tried to stop the bleeding. I thought something was wrong with me. I kept blotting the blood with toilet paper, but it wouldn't go away. When I got home that day after school, I approached my auntie.

"I'm bleeding down there, and it won't stop."

"Davinder, don't worry. It's something very normal and natural. It happens to all girls at some point. Some get it a little bit later, but it can happen starting at this age, and it's just your body going through changes," she explained reassuringly.

She quickly talked to my mum and returned with something wrapped in a paper bag.

"Here, take this." She handed it to me. "It's a sanitary pad. Just peel off the paper and line it in your underwear. Just be sure to change it every three to four hours, or whenever it becomes really drenched," she explained. Thankfully, my auntie was able to help me through that traumatic event!

My grandma played a big part in looking after us when we were little. I loved my grandma a lot. She was always nice and gentle toward us, even though she didn't always stick up for me. She was a fabulous cook and enjoyed making food for all her family members. We called my grandma *Bibi Ji*, which could mean mother or grandmother, and she called me "Bindi," my Indian nickname. She said *putt* a lot, which was a nice, endearing word that showed affection.

"*Tu meri putt ya,*" she often said. Translated, it means, "You're my darling."

Bibi Ji was quite slender and tied her gray hair back or in a bun at the back of her head. She always seemed happy and often had a smile on her face. She wore glasses and was house proud, but more than that, she was very hospitable. She took care of any visitor who walked through her door, making sure they had a good cup of tea with snacks, if not an entire meal, all handmade by her.

"Tea? I make tea", she stated to any visitor, even handymen who stopped by to fix something. Without waiting for the answer, *Bibi Ji* went ahead and made tea.

"You don't have to, Grandma," the visitor often responded. "I don't want to make you go to all that effort." For some reason, most visitors just called her "Grandma" too—perhaps because of her age, or perhaps it was their way of giving or showing her respect.

"Me like to. Tea is good," *Bibi Ji* answered with a very happy and content look, taking pride in the fact she had looked after her visitor well. She was the best hostess.

She didn't speak much English, so we spoke to her in Punjabi. Sometimes, she used one-word or short responses in English such as "yes" or "no" or "No speak English." I know *Bibi Ji* understood a lot of English but did not want to speak it, or perhaps she just couldn't use it fluently.

Bibi Ji lived with her husband, *Baba Ji*, before they separated. He scowled at us, frightening us with his glares and the nasty things he said. He didn't seem to like seeing us happy. When he saw us playing together, he yelled at us because we were having fun. He was mean to everyone, including my grandma. He was quite scary and never pleasant. She finally moved in with one of her sons—my uncle—who lived about a ten-minute walk from us.

My parents bought a Spar shop up the road from our Bradford home when I was eleven, and we moved into an apartment above it. I'm not sure if Spar exists anymore, but it was popular back then. We sold alcohol, cigarettes, and newspapers, as well as general groceries. Our living room, kitchen, bathroom, and my mum's bedroom were on the floor right above the shop, and there were two rooms on another floor above that one. One room was for my sisters and me, while the other belonged to Mandeep.

We got a puppy named Rebel after we moved into the shop. I absolutely loved our half Labrador-half Alsatian. He was black with a white chest, and I loved taking him for walks. He was allowed to be upstairs when we first got him, and he used to run around the living room. It wasn't long before he had to be downstairs in the backroom of the shop, close to the back yard. We used to give Rebel all our leftover food, whether it was sausage, chips, crisps, or our leftover *chapattis*.

Rebel spent a lot of time tied up outside in our back yard, and he wagged his tail when I watched him from the upstairs window. I used to rush out to see him and give him great big hugs, and he excitedly barked and wagged his tail. After all, I was the main one who fed him and took him for walks. I believe he liked me the most as well, as Rebel growled at Mandeep when he playfully kicked me. He was protective of me, and I grew very attached to him.

When I was sixteen, Rebel had to be looked after while my family and I went to India. I didn't realize I wouldn't see Rebel again once we returned. He had been given away to a shelter while we were out of the country for six weeks. I never understood why we couldn't get him back. My heart broke! All I could think was, *Poor Rebel … what must he be thinking?* I figured he felt we had abandoned him after having him from the time he was a baby. I will never forget his soulful eyes looking up at me while I stared at him through the hallway window.

Even though we were an Indian family who stuck to many traditions—we went to the Sikh Temple every Sunday, listened to Hindi songs and watched Bollywood movies, and wore our colorful Indian outfits to parties and weddings—we were just like any other family in England. We ate British food, watched British programs—*Coronation Street*, *Emmerdale Farm*, and *Crossroads*—and listened to British music as much as we listened to Hindi music. We often wore jeans and blouses or sweaters too. We were as much British as we were Indian.

My siblings and I were born in England. As proud as we are of being Indian, we are also extremely proud of being British and were part of the British culture we were allowed to embrace. We absorbed Western norms and ideals. This is critical to the understanding of who I was and how I was thrown into a culture that, even though I belonged to it, some of those traditions didn't exactly fit in with how and where we were raised.

We took family trips like many other British families. We went to Birmingham, which is where my dad's sister lived. We also went on a family outing to Blackpool when I was about seven or eight. My dad took lots of photos with his Polaroid camera. We were so excited to see them within moments and hold the actual pictures in our hands. To this day, I love photography and take way too many pictures!

We walked up the main street and ate fish and chips. Fish and chips from England are so tasty. We smelled their deliciousness as their very fried essence permeated the air. Most people want them once they smell the tantalizing aromas of potato and fish mixed with salt and vinegar. They were served from newspaper back in those days. Of course, there was greaseproof paper between the newspaper and the food to keep the ink off the food. We poured vinegar all over our fish and chips and dipped them in ketchup.

People visited to get away for the day or make a vacation of it for a few days. There were hotels, cafés, and restaurants galore. Blackpool had bright lights, rides, amusements, and so many shops and restaurants. It was a happy place. We saw the Blackpool Tower and the lovely seaside consisting of a very sandy beach and never-ending ocean. The fish and chips always tasted better by the sea.

My youngest auntie, who is just two years older than me, came with us on that day trip to Blackpool. We packed chai in a flask and had *parantha*, an Indian fried bread that is served with a pickle. These kinds of snacks and chai were always packed for long road trips. The drive to Blackpool must have been about an hour and a half and was considered a long road trip in England. Outside of this trip, I can't really remember too many actual leisure trips. We mostly visited family or attended weddings; that's why Blackpool was so special.

Family Secrets

Even though Kuljeet and I were put in the cellar, it was different for Mandeep. He didn't get in trouble for not doing work—he wasn't expected to work.

"He's a boy, he doesn't have to do housework like you girls," my mum admonished if we complained. "It's the job of girls to do housework and chores like this. The boy provides for the family by going out to work, the woman stays home and looks after the kids and the house."

I didn't question my mum's views on this at the time, but now when I think back to it, I know it doesn't make sense. She had to go out to work and didn't just stay home. Perhaps that's what she wanted or was the traditional way. I'm not sure why she said it but didn't live up to what she was saying.

Mandeep stayed out late and did other things my mum disapproved of, such as smoking. My brother also took a train somewhere, and my dad had to bring him back. He had run away. There was always a lot of drama in our house.

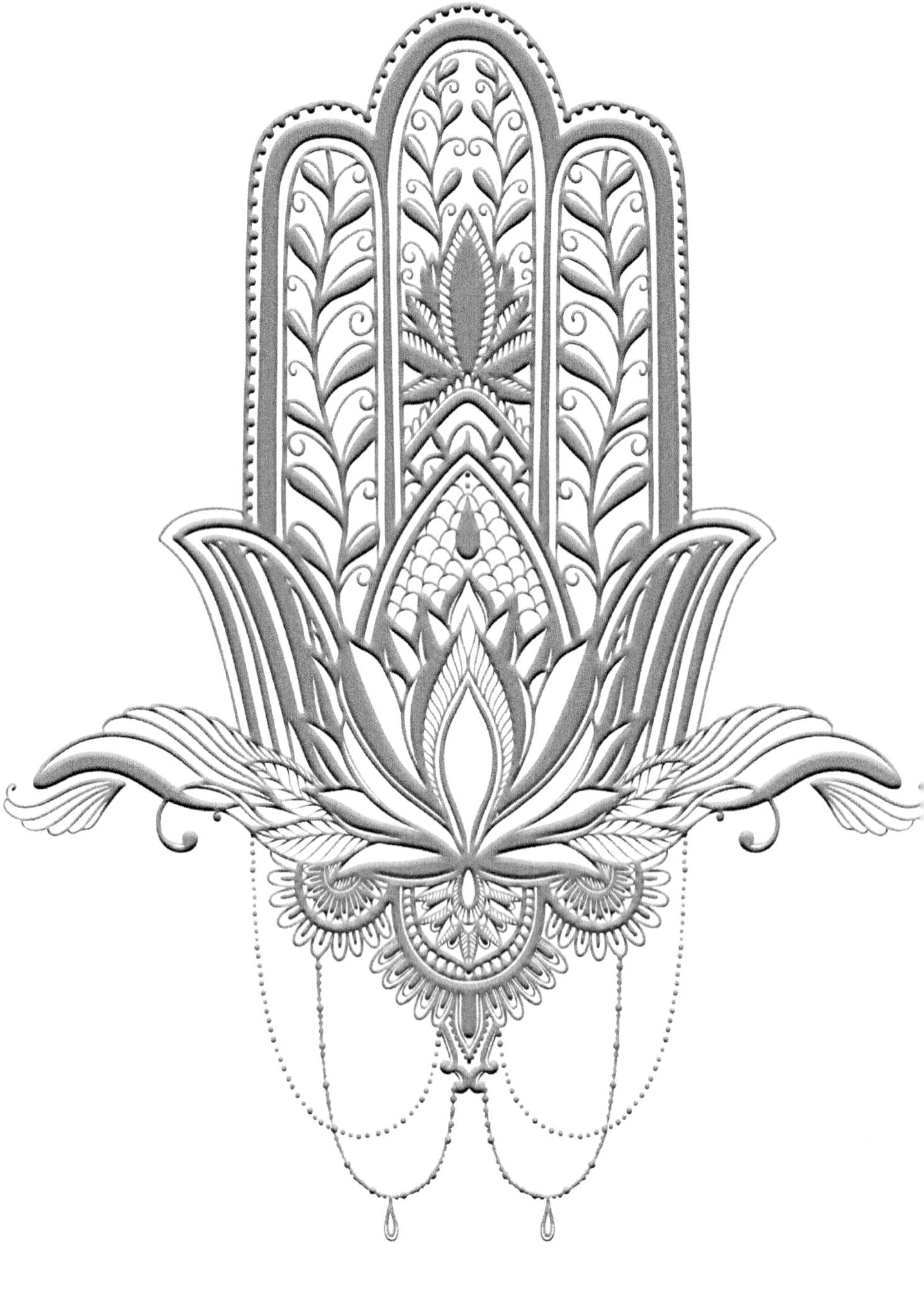

The Shop in Bradford

I walked from my high school to the shop at lunchtime and quickly made lunches for Mum and myself. I ran her food down to her so she could eat in the back room adjacent to the shop floor while I took over the register. Mandeep went to a different school farther away and didn't come home for lunch. He was already in high school, or what we called upper school in England, and had started a year before me. Sabina was much younger and in preschool. Kuljeet attended middle school and ate in the school cafeteria.

My mum ran the shop by herself all day, and I covered for her during lunches. Mandeep helped in the evenings while Mum stocked and cleaned the shop, and I cooked the meals upstairs. Kuljeet took care of her tasks in the kitchen and helped clean the shop. It was hard balancing school, working the shop, and keeping up with household chores, but it was all very necessary. It never crossed my mind to complain—we just pitched in because it was expected. My siblings and I wanted to assist whenever we were able. We were raised this way: to be helpful, not to question, and not to challenge.

I made a lot of tea, whether it was for visitors who came over or for my mum or brother. I made English tea if it was for my brother or mum, or Indian tea if it was for guests. I loved the taste of Indian tea, but it took longer to make. I had to fill a pan with water and add sugar, tea bags, cardamom, cloves, ginger, and cinnamon. Once it came to a boil, I added milk and let it return to a boil and then turned it on low heat so it would become creamier. I poured the tea through a strainer to catch the tea bags and cardamom shells, and then I had to scour and wash the pan. English tea was a lot easier, as it just involved boiling the water and steeping the tea (often in the cup itself), then adding some milk. I constantly took cups of tea down for one of them in the shop. When visitors came over, my mum went upstairs to sit with them in the living room while my brother covered for her in the shop.

I heard some of the conversation when I took in the tea, and it was always tidbits of gossiping.

"Gurpreet's daughter's wedding has been arranged to the boy from Chandigarh. Remember him? He visited here two months ago. Gurpreet is showing off his picture to everyone. She's so excited," one auntie rambled to my mum. Jindie was a big, jolly woman who wore a yellow dress over baggy yellow pants with green embroidery at the bottom and a green scarf, known as a *chunni*.

"No, I can't believe it! You mean Balbir? Balbir's wedding has been arranged already? She's just about Davinder's age. Well, if the arrangement is good, it's to be expected. Good for Gurpreet!" my mum stated approvingly.

"Yes, Gurpreet did really well by fixing her daughter's wedding to that boy. They say he is really smart, and quite good-looking." Jindie slurped the tea and smacked her lips in delight. "Hmmm, hmmmm, hmmmm. This is the best tea I've ever had. It has so much taste; I love the flavor! Hmmmmm, hmmmmm, hmmmm! Preeto, did Davinder make this?"

"Yes, Jindie, Davinder is getting really good at making tea. Hey, Davinder, pass Jindie another samosa, please."

"Here, Auntie Ji, here's another samosa for you." I had to call these women "auntie" or "Auntie Ji." "Ji" was a word we had to use after auntie or uncle (and many other titles), as it adds respect.

Every time I delivered the tea, I felt like my mum was showing her friends that her daughters were being brought up the right way: being respectful, obedient, and doing their duty—serving family. It was instilled in us to serve family first and foremost. This was the only time I ever got complimented by my mum in front of her friends, especially if they liked the tea or snacks I had made.

"Hmmmmmn, hmmmmmn, hmmmmmn," Jindie chanted as she licked her fingers. "These samosas are the best!" she raved.

The room smelled of ginger, cloves, cardamon, and cinnamon. These fragrant scents emanated from the tea—homemade Indian tea I had learned to perfect from making so often. I really did make the best tea!

My mum asked for another cup of tea for Jindie and herself, and after refilling their cups, I was expected to sit with them. I usually wasn't involved in the conversations, and sometimes my sisters joined me. We all sat to one side of the room and played a game such as Ludo, which is a board game, or we sat quietly reading our books.

We couldn't help but overhear the conversations, and we looked at each other and made funny faces when something crazy was said, which was just about every time! Inevitably, it was these kinds of talks that must have heavily influenced my mum in the steps she was about to take very soon.

Davinder Kaur

Mandeep worked in the shop but didn't do anything in the kitchen. My sisters and I made his meals and tea because boys weren't expected to do household chores. I don't think my brother even knew where we kept the cups. He used to call on the intercom that buzzed upstairs into our living room and simply say, "I would like a cup of tea, please."

I did a lot of cooking and preparation. I felt like I was in the kitchen all the time. I liked to turn on the radio and listen and dance to music from Madonna, Wham, Duran Duran, Depeche Mode, Boy George, and many other memorable pop icons. It was a way for me to escape the drudgery of my time in the kitchen and make it more enjoyable. I visualized myself on one of the popular television shows called *Top of the Pops* which had a countdown of the top-ten best songs, and everyone waited to see what number one was. When Madonna's song was announced, I imagined I was her. I got lost in another world and danced and grooved. Sometimes, all that singing and dancing contributed to me being slower in the kitchen because I lost track of time.

At first, it didn't bother me to do so much in the kitchen because I was raised to believe it was expected of all young girls. I began to question it when I started to see the injustice in it. It wasn't just about making tea and meals for my brother; I soon realized there were double standards.

Mandeep was allowed to play outside and hang out with his friends when I wasn't permitted to do the same. He went out at night, but I was required to stay home. And even though he was older, he didn't have to get married first. He was allowed to go to college if he had wanted to, but I wasn't given that option. However, my brother did an enormous amount of work in the shop. Just as girls were expected to learn cooking and cleaning skills to utilize in our new homes after our marriage, my brother was gaining experience that enabled him to become a skilled businessman when he became an adult.

Music always played in our house. If we weren't listening to English music on the kitchen radio, the radio played downstairs in the shop. We had our radiogram on during the weekends. The wooden radiogram was a beautiful piece of furniture. A record player took up one side of the rectangular surface, and the other side held all the albums in their colorful sleeves. We had a mixture of music ranging from Bollywood songs to English pop music, including The Bee Gees, Wham, The Beatles, and many others. On the weekends, my mum played Bollywood music after she had done her daily prayers. The music of my childhood formed some of my fondest memories of life back at home. I felt happiest when I listened to music.

First thing in the morning, my mum played the religious songs and said her prayers. She read from the *Guru Granth Sahib*—the religious scripture of Sikhism—and covered her hair with a *chunni*. We knew not to interrupt her while she prayed.

When music wasn't playing, we had our television on. We always had some type of background noise, and even to this day, I am soothed by it. From the moment I wake up and go into the living room, I turn on the television for comfort. It's interesting how some habits from our childhood become ingrained into our everyday lives as an adult.

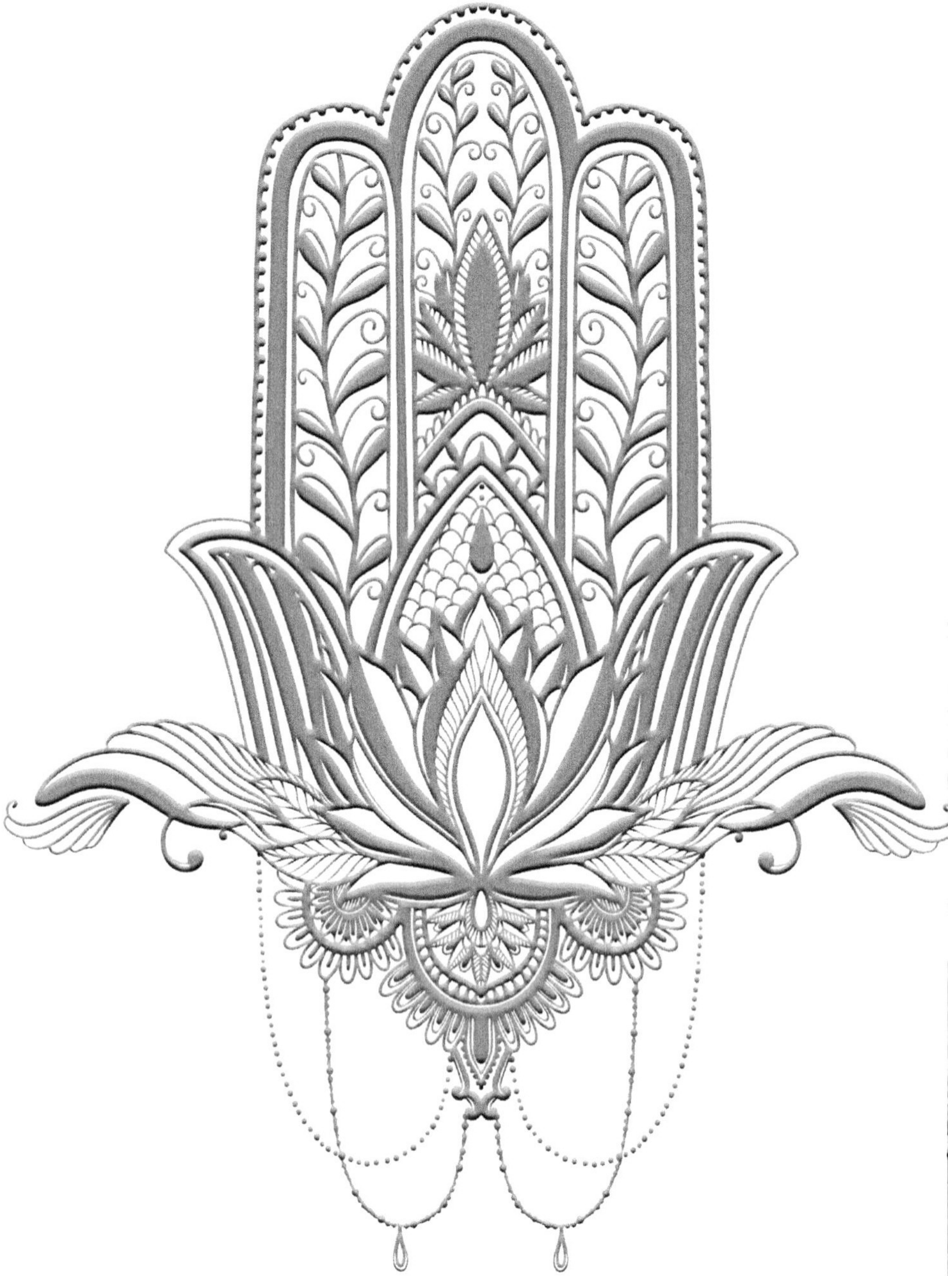

Community

We were expected to go to the *gurudwara*—the Indian Sikh temple—almost every Sunday. My brother didn't have the same expectation and made it clear he didn't want to go, and my mum was okay with that. She was lenient regarding my brother, but if we said we didn't want to go, we weren't allowed to stay home. My mum took us, but sometimes we went with my grandma.

First, we went to the kitchen in the basement and had tea and snacks. My mum gathered with the community members for their weekly gossip sessions and relayed the stories to us when we got home. No one was able to get away from prying eyes in Bradford. The people had nothing better to do than poke their nose into other people's business and talk about them. It was their full-time hobby.

"Oh, did you hear that Nadia went off with the Pakistani boy? Make sure you keep your daughters away from those Pakistanis. They are bad news! They're only after our Indian girls to disrespect them and get them pregnant, and then they leave them and get married to the Pakistani wife their parents found for them. Meanwhile, who is ever going to want the Indian girl who got pregnant from the Pakistani boy?" one woman said.

"No one! Poor Nadia's mum. It's no wonder I haven't seen her at the temple for two weeks now! I heard from Balbinder that Nadia's mum is so distraught and cries hysterically!" another replied.

How my Indian neighbors in Bradford interacted with my mum really set the stage for how we had to behave in public. She was very strict with us because of their gossiping. They apparently saw and knew everything that was going on, so my mum instilled a fear in us of always being careful of what we did. She told my sisters and I not to let the Pakistani boys—or *any* boys—approach us, and we were not to get into their cars. She went on and on about their mission to corrupt us and destroy our lives. She said they picked on Indian girls instead of Pakistani girls because they wanted to target us. The Pakistani boys drove up and down the streets outside our high school and whistled and cat-called the girls. Some of the girls loved the attention and got into their cars just to show off to their friends.

After having snacks and tea, we went upstairs to the main room. *Baba Ji* was the priest. This name is not to be confused with my grandfather because *Baba Ji* can be the name given to the father, grandfather, and priests. It's an honorific name given to show respect. *Baba Ji* prayed, and we did our *Matha Tek* by putting our heads to the ground and bowing down to God and/or the Gurus. We then sat and observed the service. At some point in the middle of the service, my mum, my grandma, my sisters, and I went downstairs to prepare food. We washed dishes and made *roti* or mixed the curries.

Seva means "to be of service to the community." We had to show we were good girls who did a lot of work. After the *langar*, when everyone came downstairs to eat after the service, we cleaned up and did the dishes again. Then, when the women were talking, the kids played in another room next to the kitchen.

School

We were never driven back and forth to school like kids are today. We walked just about everywhere, even to Bradford City Centre. It was only a twenty-minute walk from our shop. Since Mum and Dad worked a lot, my grandma arrived early in the morning and walked us the ten minutes to her house, where we waited a little while before our aunties and my grandma escorted us to school.

My mum and her two younger sisters are fifteen and seventeen years apart. In fact, Mum was pregnant with my brother a year after my grandma had her youngest daughter. My mum also has two younger brothers—one is a couple of years younger and the other was five years younger. Unfortunately, her youngest brother lost his battle with cancer a few years ago.

My mum's sisters are close to me in age—one is two years older and the other is about four years older. The oldest attended the middle school, and the youngest was next door at the elementary school with me. We've always gotten along very well. The oldest likes to joke around and is very easy to talk to, and the youngest is a very jovial and fun-loving woman.

I spent most of my early childhood surrounded by extended family such as my two aunties, my two uncles, and their kids. We had a lot of family, and we often got together for birthdays and weddings.

The Culture and Tradition

I was allowed to walk to school with friends when I was in high school. Back then, I didn't realize it as freedom, but I do now. I appreciate that I was given this opportunity to walk with my friends. One of my friends was from Hong Kong. In the mornings, we met at her family's fish and chip shop and walked to school together.

I came home from high school for lunch, walked back, and then returned home again. Sometimes, I walked with one of my Indian friends who lived across the street from me. Kaljit had strict parents and did everything perfectly, as we all did at that age. She was the only girl but had an older brother. Later, I found out Kaljit had violated our strict Indian code of behavior by going off with one of the Pakistani boys. He left her after she got pregnant. Her parents disowned her, and I'm not sure where Kaljit is and what happened to her.

We sometimes stopped by at another friend's house on the way to school. Daljinder was another very obedient girl who never stepped out of line. Her parents were a little less strict but still traditional. I wish I had been able to stay in contact with all these girls from my childhood, but I ended up losing touch because I moved to Hull and then out of the country.

My girlfriends from school met the same fate I did. We all had arranged marriages planned for us when we were only fourteen years old. We never questioned our parents. We thought it was normal because it was part of our culture. Arranged marriages are forced marriages when one or both of the parties don't want to go ahead with it. Since a child is too young to give proper consent to a marriage when they are fourteen, they are being taken advantage of. They do not understand what is happening to them. When they realize it years later, they can't get out of the arrangement because it's already been several years into the agreement. When an arranged marriage turns out to be a forced marriage, that's an abuse of human rights. It's human trafficking, as well as slavery. This kind of early planning of a child's life is not to be tolerated. Abuse should not be a part of anyone's culture, yet it continues to happen in the name of culture and tradition. Arranged marriage is abuse when it involves coercion. Indian people—and Pakistanis, Turkish, Saudi Arabians, Lebanese, and most African countries, to name just a few—engage in arranged marriage as a form of cultural practice or tradition. This has gone on for years, and people would like for these traditions to continue. Some traditions don't work and shouldn't exist anymore. Traditions that involve abuse should be stopped.

My mum was a child bride. She and my dad had an arranged marriage when she was seventeen. People who follow this tradition get their children married young so they are set with a union approved by the family. Early marriages are encouraged to keep children from making poor decisions and to prevent the boys from sidetracking the girls and making the wrong choices. It also alleviates the risk of marrying someone from another nationality, religion, or even caste.

If a girl had a relationship with a boy outside of marriage, it was considered a major afront to her family. It was even worse if she married him without approval from her parents or got pregnant out of wedlock. The parents worried most about what the community might think if their daughter became pregnant. After that was the concern of whether the girl could ever be marriage material after causing such a scandal.

It seemed that conforming to the expectations of our community and society was most important to parents like mine. We had to heed to expectations and norms. I know my grandma must have also had a child marriage because this tradition is passed from one generation to the next. People must learn to break this cycle of abuse and not perpetuate traditions that don't make sense. In my opinion, it can never make sense to marry a girl to a stranger and put her in danger. If either person isn't happy with the arranged marriage, which may have been a forced marriage, there will be unhappiness and resentment. When these negative emotions exist, either person could become angry—sometimes, it's both parties. This frequently results in domestic violence. My mum often talked about the abuse from my dad, but she never really talked about how she felt getting married to him at an early age.

It's important to clarify that arranged marriages are *thought* to occur when both parties consent, whereas one or both parties don't want the marriage in a forced marriage. As I continue to relay my story, I want to make it clear that not all arranged marriages involve the consent of both parties like they're supposed to. When it comes to forced marriages, not all children who are experiencing these arrangements know the term "forced marriage" or question what their parents are doing, trusting that their parents have their best interests at heart for them.

Children only know the term "arranged marriage" because they are brought up being told this is part of their culture and tradition. They are gaslit and manipulated into thinking and believing their parents will always look out for their best interests. They don't dream of questioning what is being planned for them.

Children need to be taught about forced marriage and how an arranged wedding *can* be a forced marriage if either party doesn't freely consent to it. No parent says to their child, "I'm arranging your forced marriage." Instead, they say, "I'm arranging your marriage." Parents are abusing their power. By arranging marriages, they are controlling their kids by enforcing traditions and culture. Children blindly trust their parents, and when they wake up with the knowledge of what is about to happen to them, it's already too late. It's a complicated and harmful process that really needs to stop. Education in the schools is critical, or kids will not realize what is happening to them. Parents will continue deceiving their kids to perpetuate traditions that have no place in this day and age.

I didn't question what was going on around me at the time. Girls were obviously getting married, and no one said anything about it. Perhaps it was because I accepted it as the norm. I now realize it's a bad tradition—one that must change. Maybe I accepted it because it was in the Hindi movies we watched. It wasn't a totally strange occurrence since I saw it all the time.

I was born into the culture, and that's why I didn't question it. However, I wasn't educated enough at that age to understand it was wrong, and neither were the other girls. We weren't old enough, mature enough, or sophisticated enough to know any better or question whether it was fair or ethical.

Why did no one bother to talk to us and ask us how we felt?

Why did no one educate us about our rights?

Perhaps human rights weren't really talked about back then. Or it's possible we weren't considered human enough for our rights to matter. I'm not sure, but it seemed that was the case.

Was it really okay to marry off girls under the age of eighteen, whether they wanted it or not, and let kids have kids?

Was it okay for a girl to be raped by her husband just because they're married?

Why is it different now versus then? If it's an abuse of human rights today, logic says it was the same back then.

Are we just waking up to human rights violations? Have we all been asleep?

Our teachers failed us, our community failed us, and our families failed us.

What about those of us who were married at eighteen? We could have been educated about our rights at fourteen or fifteen. Our teachers could have told us we didn't have to follow tradition or culture. We should have been able to *choose* our spouses when we *wanted* to take that step in our lives. It doesn't make it okay just because we were married off at eighteen. The fact that many of us were shown pictures at the age of fourteen of the spouses we had to marry at eighteen made us child marriage victims. We were given a prison sentence in the form of an engagement. We couldn't get out of the arrangement because we had already been engaged for *four years.* From the time we were fourteen, we were spoken for and had become someone else's property. Kids should be kids, not brides or grooms!

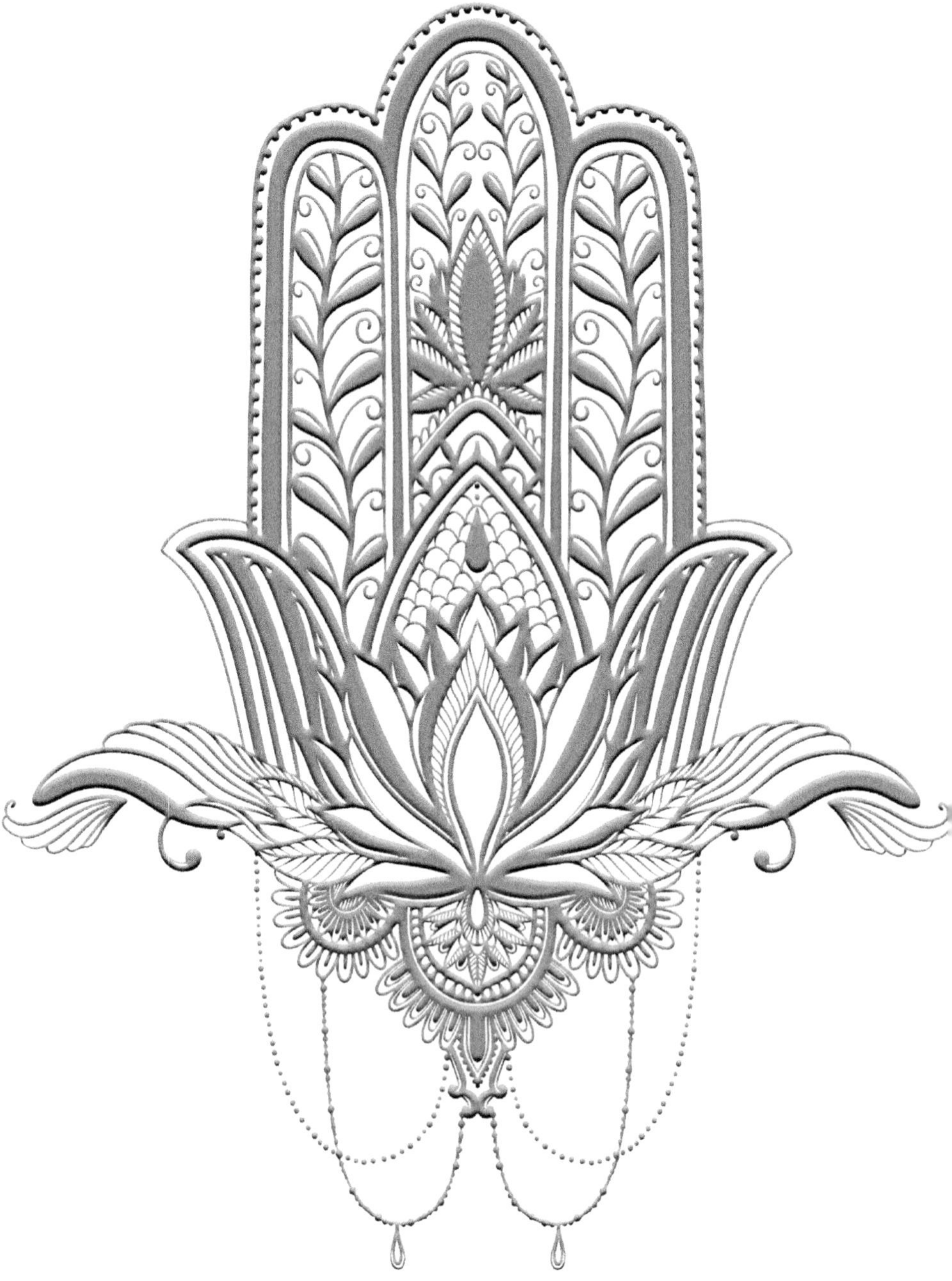

The Picture

When I was fourteen, we received a visitor when I was in the back room of the shop with my mum. Mr. Shergill was a traditional Sikh man who wore large turbans and was kind of big himself. He intimidated me, and I flinched when I saw him. I think I considered any Punjabi man with a turban as being strict and very religious. It was an effort for me to play the part of the polite girl, which was my given role whether I wanted it or not. I was expected to smile, not argue, not question, and to quickly ask whether someone wanted some tea. Just because I was a little frightened of Mr. Shergill did not give me the right to avoid my duty. If I didn't do what was expected of me, I was meant to suffer the consequences.

"So, Davinder, how are you today?"

"I am doing well, Mr. Shergill. Can I get some tea for you?"

"Yes, please. That would be really nice! Thank you."

I didn't *want* to make tea for him because it would prolong his stay at our house.

Mr. Shergill seemed to like me. He had his eyes set on me for a boy from the Punjab in India. He and my mum were busy talking when I came back downstairs with the tray of tea and snacks. They whispered and looked over at me occasionally. He handed a photo to my mum, and she immediately showed it to me.

"This is a really nice boy. You are very lucky to get a chance to marry this kind of boy. He is good-looking and well-educated. What do you think? Do you say yes?"

I didn't really understand what was going on. All I knew was that my friends were getting arranged weddings too—all the girls had to. We never were allowed to date boys. We had no say in it. We were to be obedient and agreeable to anything our elders arranged for us.

My mum frequently talked about "this girl" or "that girl" who was already engaged, and I know she would have slapped me across the face, or worse, if I dared to question the choice. Deep down, I knew what she'd say if I argued.

"Who do you think you are? So-and-so had an arranged marriage and didn't say no to her mum. Your friend also had her wedding arranged, and the boy is from India. What's so special about *you*? What makes *you* so different?"

With every fiber of my being, I knew we had no say when it came to marriage decisions. No choices. No voice. Many times, we were supposed to be there and be quiet. We looked nice as a decoration, as we worked in the background, but our voices or thoughts weren't important. It only mattered that we washed dishes quicker than each other, cleaned better than each other, and did more work than anyone else. Gaslighting and abuse were deeply embedded in my experience.

My mum knew nothing of the boy in the picture, but she was excited. She was able to begin planning weddings for her four kids, and even though I wasn't the eldest, I was the first to be married. She probably found out as much as she needed to know, like his name, age, and that he had family in Birmingham, where his brother lived.

After Mr. Shergill left, my mum turned to me. "What do you think of the boy? He's good-looking, isn't he?"

I nodded shyly because I didn't know what else to do or say.

"Do you agree?" she asked for the second time. She had already asked in front of Mr. Shergill, and I had said yes because I knew I couldn't say no. How could I say no now?

"Yes, I agree, Mum."

I think I was too young to understand what engagement and marriage *really* meant, but that wasn't the question. I'd said yes. I had to.

I was just a child and didn't know what I was getting into, but now my heart aches for my fourteen-year-old self. I wish I could help her and tell her to be strong and say no. But that teenage girl was obedient and not the girl she is now. Older. Wiser.

That younger me should have been allowed to choose. She was robbed of the freedom to say "no" without repercussions. No child should be faced with such an inappropriate question, much less be forced to answer it. My human rights were stolen from me at the age of fourteen because I was officially engaged and someone else's property. I was spoken for.

It all happened so quickly. How can *any* fourteen-year-old know saying yes meant she was limiting her choices and her freedom? There was no backing out of it at a later stage. From the moment I agreed, I was trapped. My nightmare had just begun.

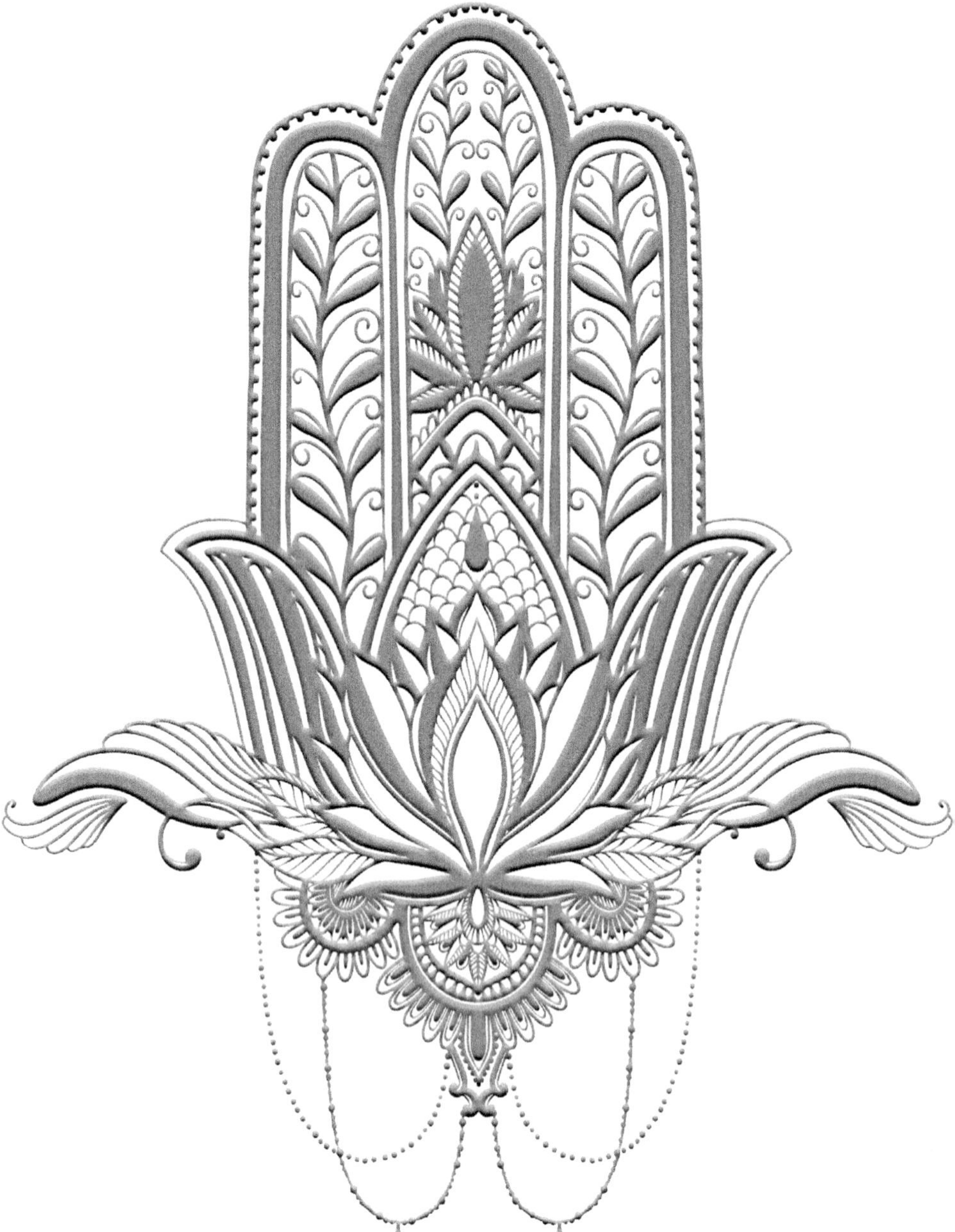

The Engagement

Within a week or so, the boy in the picture was in England. We made the ten-minute walk to meet with the boy at my youngest uncle's house. He was the least strict of my mum's two brothers.

I wore an Indian outfit and had my hair pulled back. I had to have my hair tied up quite a lot back then. To have it down and styled would have made me look more attractive, so that was out of the question. We were always told not to doll ourselves up until we were married. Makeup wasn't necessary, nor allowed, and we weren't permitted to wear dresses or skirts unless they were part of our school uniform when we were in middle school. In high school, we were permitted to wear whatever we wanted to within reason, except for skirts, dresses, and anything questionable or inappropriate. The last two were the school's rules, and it was safe to say they were all part of my mum's rules too. Usually, my sisters and I wore jeans or pants with tops. We wore Indian outfits on the weekends or to special events such as weddings or parties. A *salwar* and *chameez*, the traditional Punjabi outfit, consisted of a long top and baggy pants. We sometimes wore tight-fitting pants called *pajame* pants.

"You can only say 'hello' to him and then just sit next to him quietly. Okay?" My mum looked at me in a very foreboding manner as though to warn me that my conduct at this time was important to get correct, and I mustn't step one foot out of line.

"Okay," I responded.

"Just look ahead most of the time and sit straight," she commanded. "You won't go wrong if you do as you're told. You will have your pictures taken with him and his family. Just smile for the camera, okay?"

"Okay, Mum," I responded not too excitedly because I was getting a little anxious. It seemed this event was important, but I didn't know why.

I did as I was told. I looked at Bik very nervously when he entered my uncle's home. I wasn't interested in seeing him because he was just another stranger. I didn't quite associate the significance of what was happening, but I did *not* like his arm around me when we posed for pictures together and with his brother and sister-in-law. I didn't know him and had not given him permission, but somehow, he acted like he had every right to do it.

That was my engagement party, but I never saw it that way until many years later when I reflected on it. The reality of everything that happened only sank in when I was nearly forty and attending university in San Diego. One day, I read on Twitter about other forced marriage victims. Jasvinder Sanghera[1] described how she ran away from a forced marriage after seeing what happened to her four older sisters who had all suffered unhappy arranged marriages. I began to draw a parallel between our experiences. My heart broke, and I felt her pain succinctly. Her pain was my pain. I cried for her and her sisters, my sister, my brother, myself, my friends, and the hundreds of thousands of girls and boys who had gone through these traumatic experiences.

---

1   Jasvinder Sanghera https://www.jasvindersanghera.com/

On that day at my uncle's house, people took pictures of us. Mr. Shergill was there, as well as the boy's brother and sister-in-law. We had a little party of sorts, with tea, samosas, and other snacks. They were all very happy, but I don't think I had any emotions about the event. It was yet another thing on a list of many things I was made to do and go along with. I had no say. Engagements were supposed to be happy and exciting, probably the most exciting time in our life other than our wedding day.

Later in life, I wondered why my engagement had to be like that and not like Princess Diana's. I still remember her wearing the famous blue outfit as she showed off the sapphire-and-diamond ring. She was the picture of happiness and had chosen her husband herself. Even though we all know how her marriage turned out, it was a fairytale romance at the time, just like the romances in the books I read every night.

What had happened to *my* chances of romance?

Apparently, I was not to be afforded the same rights as the characters in my books. I had to sit next to a stranger and pose for pictures, play-acting and smiling for the cameras. Pretending to be happy. Unfortunately, this became a pattern in my life.

I typically call him "the boy" when I speak of Bik. I can't quite explain it. I feel I shouldn't give him the respect of naming him. Perhaps he was just as much a victim of our parents arranging our marriage as I was, but for some reason, I felt like he wanted it. After all, he had a lot more to gain from it than I did. It gave him the chance to move from India and be in England, close to his brother. I'm not sure if his brother sponsoring his immigration to England was even an option. I assume it wasn't because the opportunity to marry me was introduced instead.

I had to talk nicely to his brother and sister-in-law and pose for photos with them as if we knew one another. They were strangers to me, and so was he—"the boy." Back then, it wasn't called a forced marriage, but I now know it had the elements of what constitutes a forced marriage. A child cannot consent!

How can any fourteen-year-old girl know what she really wants? How can she say yes to marriage when she should have the opportunity to enjoy her childhood and *then* choose who she wants to marry, when she wants to marry them?

The boy was average-looking and kind of short, although my mum described him as being tall. I vaguely recall he wore a suit of some sort that day. I wasn't allowed to look at him, and my mum kept the photo. If I'm being honest, I didn't want it. My mum said he was handsome, but I certainly didn't find him attractive when I was fourteen, when I saw him in India a year later, and again when I was eighteen—the third time we met.

It deeply disturbs me that *children* are forced into situations like mine. I had a picture taken with a boy, was only allowed to say "hello" and pose for a few photos, and my fate was sealed. Voilà … we were engaged!

I knew something wasn't right. I was supposed to experience romance, dating, and falling in love. My books had painted images of joy, laughter, and warm feelings when it came to relationships, but all of that meant nothing in my world. The characters in my books and television shows were fictional, but there were elements of truth and parallels to the "real world" in their stories.

What had I done to deserve to be deprived of that which so many others had in abundance?

Writing and Calling

The boy went back to India after a few weeks, but Mr. Shergill visited us quite often. He was a *bachola*—a middleman—who arranged weddings or found matches for someone's son or daughter. What made him think the boy was suitable for me? He was from India, and I was from England. Sure, both of us are Indian, but Eastern and Western values are stark in contrast. I mentioned earlier that I watched British television shows, listened to British pop music, and read romance books that were in English and mostly based in the West. Of course, I was very much Westernized, even though I had some Eastern values instilled in me. I was more British than Indian, and I felt more connected to Western culture than Eastern culture. This is typical for children who are born and raised in a country far away from where their parents were born and raised. I don't think Mr. Shergill or my parents thought about this. I flinch when I think of the matchmaker who was partly responsible for ruining my life.

Bik's brother and sister-in-law really liked me, and I liked them too. They seemed very nice. My mum often wanted me to talk to them on the phone, but I didn't enjoy it. What was there to talk about? I had nothing in common with them, the boy, or anyone else in their family.

When they visited our home, I was required to impress them with my domestic skills by making tea and a great lunch or dinner consisting of a vegetable curry, a meat curry, and *chapattis* I made from scratch.

I was also encouraged to talk to the boy on the phone. I certainly didn't like that. I mostly replied with yes or no answers to avoid conversing with him.

"Hello, this is Bik", he said in Punjabi.

"Hello, how are you? I replied politely.

"I am well. What have you been up to?"

"Nothing much." I couldn't conjure up more of a sentence in Punjabi without a lot of effort, and it would have been broken Punjabi.

There were many pauses in our conversation, and it was really awkward. We didn't have anything to talk about, and we had nothing in common because we didn't know each other. I didn't *want* to get to know him.

"Would you like to talk to my mum?" I prayed he would say yes.

"Okay, it was nice talking to you. Bye, Davinder."

"Bye." I handed the phone to my mum as quickly as I could.

After my mum finished talking to him, I tried to tell her how I felt.

"Mum, I don't want to talk to him. There is nothing to talk about."

"You have to talk to him. He misses you," Mum said.

"How can he miss me? He doesn't even know me. I don't know him," I cautiously responded, afraid I had said something she was going to take issue with.

"Of course, he misses you. He's been waiting to marry you all this time. He wants to get to know you. You need to get to know him." Mum looked at me sharply.

I knew she didn't want an argument. Her glance reminded me I needed to proceed very cautiously with what I said next.

"Well, I can't speak Punjabi properly with him."

"Whose fault is that? You can speak Punjabi if you really try. You are Indian, after all, not English, and you need to be able to speak your language," she snapped.

"Okay, I'll try." I knew I wasn't going to get anywhere with my mum. I had to talk to the boy every now and then. I just hoped he wouldn't call very often, and I certainly wouldn't call him, unless I was forced to.

He had spent fifteen minutes or so with me that day at my uncle's house. Even then, we hardly conversed with each other and just said hello. Also, I didn't want to get to know him, and why would I? I wasn't excited about him or looking forward to our marriage. To me, it was a distant event for when I was eighteen, which was the legal age for marriage in the United Kingdom. Additionally, I felt very self-conscious speaking Punjabi because we spoke mostly English at home on a day-to-day basis. My mum and dad occasionally spoke Punjabi, but we answered in English. I sometimes used Punjabi, but not as often as English. I spoke it when we were at the Sikh Temple or with other family members, such as my aunties and grandparents. Now that I live in the United States, my Punjabi is getting rusty, and I hardly speak it at all. I still understand it, and it comes back, but it's certainly not fluent.

My mum encouraged me to write letters to him. I wrote one or two brief notes in which I had to make false statements such as, "I miss you and can't wait until you come here." I didn't think about it back then, but posing with him for pictures created a façade—like I was happy. I was not. I was told what to do, what to say, and how to behave.

I was, in essence, a robot.

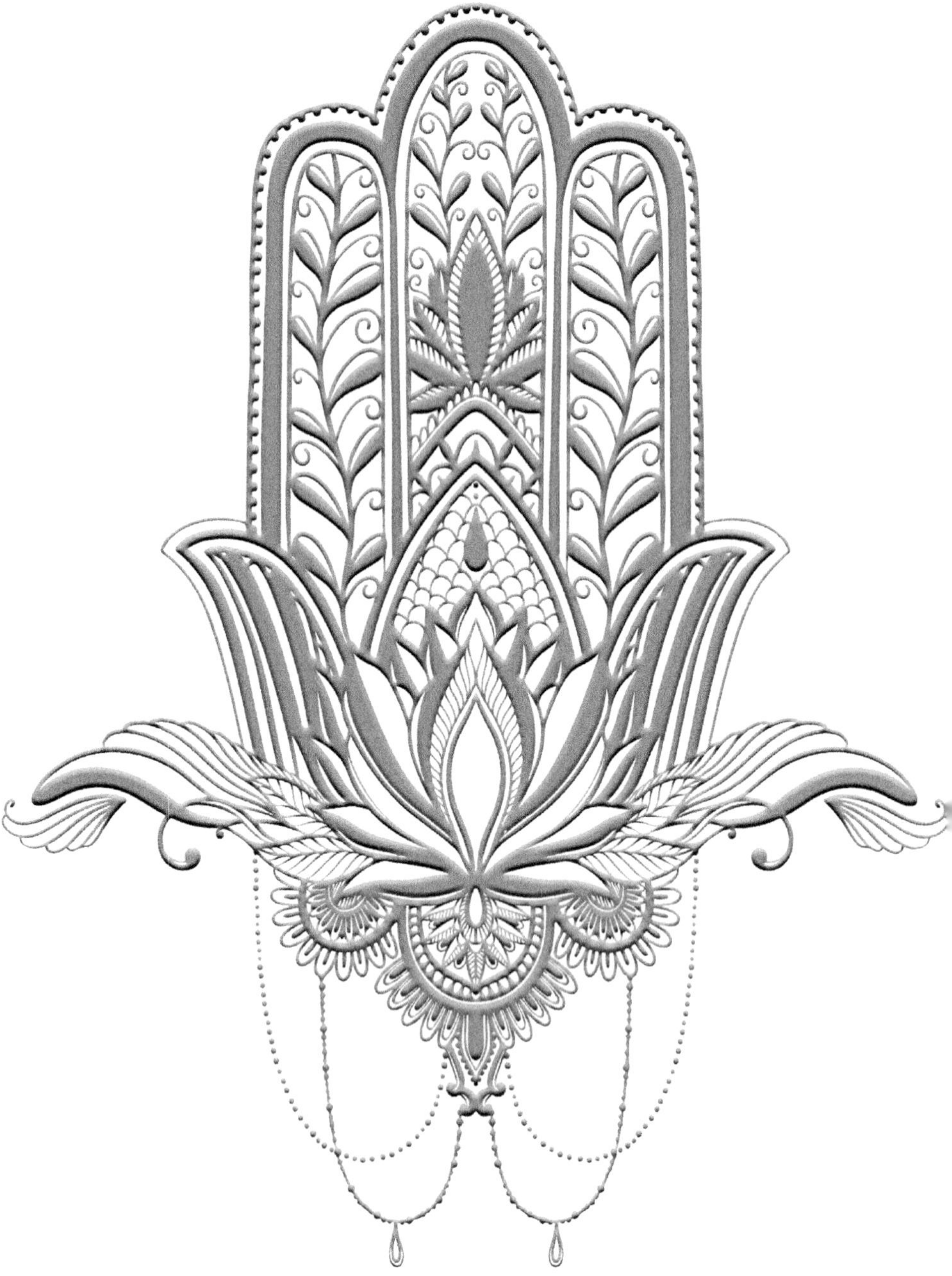

1985 Trip to India

During a six-week summer holiday from school, my family and I traveled to India to stay with relatives in the Punjab. While standing in line to show our passports at the Delhi airport, I began to feel faint.

"Mum, I'm not feeling good. I'm getting dizzy again."

She appeared as though she wanted to shut me up and I was bothering her. It was the kind of look that said, "Do not bother me right now. I am burdened by many things. Can't you see? Don't you have any sense?" My mum ignored me after giving me the special face treatment—her cold, hostile, and angry expression.

It wasn't long before I passed out and woke up on the ground.

I got dizzy quite often when I was younger, especially when I stood for too long. I hadn't been drinking enough water and had very little sodium in my diet, but that diagnosis didn't come until later. However, at the time, my mum never bothered to take it seriously or ask the doctors for help. Apparently, I was just being a nuisance at the airport that day. My welcome to India had already been tainted with bad luck.

Initially, my siblings and I didn't like India. Our friends back home spent summer holidays in Spain or France, but we were in a place without indoor toilets. If we needed to use the restroom, we took a jug of water and walked to the fields—day *and* night. I was extremely bothered by the lack of privacy. And forget about toilet paper; that's what the water was for. I'll never forget the pungent odor and being careful to avoid stepping on someone else's defecation. We got used to it after a while, believe it or not, but I never took toilets for granted again.

India was hot and *very* different from England. The electricity went out a lot, and there were none of the modern conveniences we took for granted at home—no microwaves, refrigerators, or washing and drying machines. A small television was inside the house, but we rarely entered the home.

We went into the house the first night and promptly ran out the door at the sight of lizards scurrying along the walls. We slept outside in the courtyard each night, but we had to contend with the mosquitoes as they buzzed all around us. The air was humid, but we covered our faces with blankets. It was difficult to breathe, almost suffocating, but we were willing to suffer if it kept the pests from biting us.

After nearly two weeks in India, I began to appreciate the simple things. I realized all the modern conveniences of my life in England weren't that necessary—except for the toilets, of course. I recognized greater rewards were attached to the simple life. Spending time with family at meals or drinking tea with one another in the courtyard increases the quality of family bonds. Not having distractions such as the television allowed us to be present in the moment and take in the entire experience.

We also went on a little side trip to Simla, which is up in the Himalayan Mountains. I loved it there, but the trip disagreed with my system. I got sick and felt strange. I believe it had something to do with the elevation, and it took a while for me to adjust to that change. It played tricks on my body, and I felt very disoriented.

We had a delightful stay in a hotel once we got settled in though. Monkeys tapped on our hotel windows in the mornings.

It was surreal. It rained one minute and was dry the next. The freshness of the earth permeated the air when the sun came out, and the aroma lingered. I enjoyed seeing the monkeys, and to this day, I love them. I've always wanted to go back to Simla, and when I visit India again, I would love to take my kids there. Our trip to Simla was important to me because it was the only part of our holiday that felt like a vacation. Otherwise, I would write off the entire India trip as being for another purpose altogether and certainly not for a family holiday.

We visited the boy's village in the Punjab, and there was another big party I didn't realize was akin to an engagement party until years later. His entire family, except his brother and sister-in-law from the UK, met me at the party, and I was introduced to his parents for the first time. No one had told me we were going to visit Bik's village. It was like I didn't need to know any details; my feelings and thoughts were of no importance.

A big table was set up on their land for lunch. There was a lot of food, and it was easy to see a great deal of effort was put into it because we were given dish after dish.

Before we sat down for the food, and after I met his parents, Bik came outside.

"Hello," he greeted me in Punjabi.

"Hello," I replied in Punjabi.

We didn't say anything else to one another at all, except for "goodbye" when we left. We had more pictures taken together and with his family. I suppose I was the guest of honor, but little did I know, this was my engagement party. The *second* one! Bik sat a few seats away from me at the table.

"Nice to meet you, and thank you for the lovely food," I said to his parents when we left.

"You are very welcome, daughter. We wish to see you again very soon." They hugged me.

Bik joined his hands together and said, "Goodbye," I did the same. I was so happy I didn't have to get close to him.

Another purpose of the trip to India was to buy clothes and jewelry for my wedding. My mum accumulated the clothes far in advance for the big day, and it was a well-known fact that it was cheaper to buy clothes from India, especially wedding clothes. Later, I realized parents use this tactic quite often. They take their children to the land of their origin under the guise of a family vacation; however, the trip is meant to facilitate arranging the marriage. I thought it was a holiday, but it was a business trip—the business of engagement and arranged marriage. I didn't realize all of this then; I just knew I was getting married, and this was what parents did.

My brother also got engaged on this trip. He certainly wasn't happy about this, but just like me, he had no say in the matter. My brother let his feelings be known, and it was obvious he didn't want to marry a girl from India.

"Mum, I don't want to get married. I'm too young," Mandeep said repeatedly. "What's the rush? I'm only seventeen! I don't want to be married to someone you find here!"

"You have to get married! You know that. This is what we do in our Indian culture. Your friends have to get married too; everyone does. You will be just fine!" My mum dismissed all his objections and feelings.

Before he knew it, a girl was chosen for him. Mum didn't let Mandeep have any say in picking his future bride. She hadn't even selected several girls for him to choose from. My brother was good-looking, and it's fair to say he was a good catch. Not only did he have pleasant attributes, but he was from the United Kingdom. That factor alone was attractive to potential brides who wanted to go abroad with hopes for a better life. It seemed my mum had picked the first available girl. It was almost like she felt she was going to run out of time, but I don't know why the choice was so rushed. It was the wrong thing to do, but if she had to do it, she could have at least put some effort into thinking about it. My mum seemed to be in a hurry to get us all engaged and married as soon as possible so she could have grandchildren.

I often wondered how Mum was able to put her wants and needs above her children's happiness and mental well-being. It likely never occurred to her to think that way on our behalf. Everyone around her arranged their children's weddings, and she saw no one rebelling.

Mum was expected to perpetuate the tradition. After all, my grandparents had gone to England when my mum was about nine years old, and my dad's parents had taken him to England when he was around ten. Their minds were frozen in the time they'd spent in India, and they carried on the traditions of the past, not realizing India itself was evolving and moving on. The people in India were much more modern than the Indians in England. My grandparents passed this on to my mum and her siblings. She not only had to fulfill the wishes of my grandparents but also those of her brothers, who were indoctrinated in my grandparents' view of life and how they thought it should be.

My mum didn't seem to know any better. She was just trying to make her dreams come true and follow the way she was brought up. The son was to be married, and his wife was meant to come into the house and help with the cooking and cleaning. The girls of the house were to be married and move away to their new in-laws' houses. My mum was going to stick to this tradition whether we wanted it or not. We were never asked. The elders planned the future, and the youngsters' wishes didn't matter. We were raised to be subservient and not argue.

Mother didn't seem to realize where a person is born and the culture they grow up with helps determine their path. I grew up in the Indian way of life, but I was also surrounded by British norms and customs. I believe culture influences what a person wants out of life. My family's traditions were a stark contrast to what I'd witnessed at school and other places outside the Indian community. Mum obviously didn't see we were at odds with the culture she bathed us in and the culture surrounding us. Even though I now realize Mum wasn't trying to harm us intentionally, we had all been tricked. We didn't seem to matter; we were just children who didn't have any say. But if we didn't matter, why arrange our weddings? When I think about the trip to India now, I count my blessings that my fate didn't turn out like so many other girls who go to India or Pakistan during the summer holidays. They don't return home; instead, they are forced into marriage while on their so-called holiday.

I was lucky compared to other girls. It feels odd to say that because no one is lucky to be forced into marriage. I wasn't forced to marry while I was in India, and I was allowed to reach the age of eighteen, even though the older age didn't make the situation any better.

A Saudi Arabian girl in my class didn't come back to school right after the summer holiday, but she was different when she finally returned. She dressed in glamorous clothing and wore makeup, a sign she had been married during the break. At fourteen, she had become a child bride, but no one questioned it.

Girls should be studying and having fun at that age, but we were robbed of our childhood. Instead, we were domesticated and trained for a life of servitude to a man and his family.

Since I've been here in America, I've heard from many Hindu Indians who have experienced arranged marriages, but they were given a choice to say no and got to see pictures of various prospects. It seems Hindus have more freedom than Punjabis. In my opinion, Punjabis are stricter.

One of my older cousins was allowed to attend college in Leeds and live on campus, away from her family. She didn't have to get married until after she graduated. Even though we're from the same family, her upbringing and expectations bore a stark contrast to mine because we lived two hours apart and in different households.

Based on my experience and observations, there are two types of Indians. There are those who want their children to be educated in order to have every chance in life. They normally want their children to become doctors, lawyers, judges, or scientists. The parents still arrange marriages to ensure their children marry someone suitable.

On the other side of the coin, there are Indians who don't care about education and only focus on marriage. They believe a woman's place is to serve her husband and his family, and that is exactly the group my family fell into. The girls with whom I attended school in Bradford seemed to have similar familial traditions. I'm not sure if the fact we were all Punjabis and had strict parents had something to do with it, but it's eerie to think an entire city of Indians in England had the exact same belief patterns.

Hindu Indians in San Diego appear to be more liberal and have adopted a relaxed set of expectations. Most of these women that I know are close to my age and came from India, but it goes to show India is more modern and advanced than certain parts of England, namely Bradford. In India, many women are also allowed to finish their education before they get married.

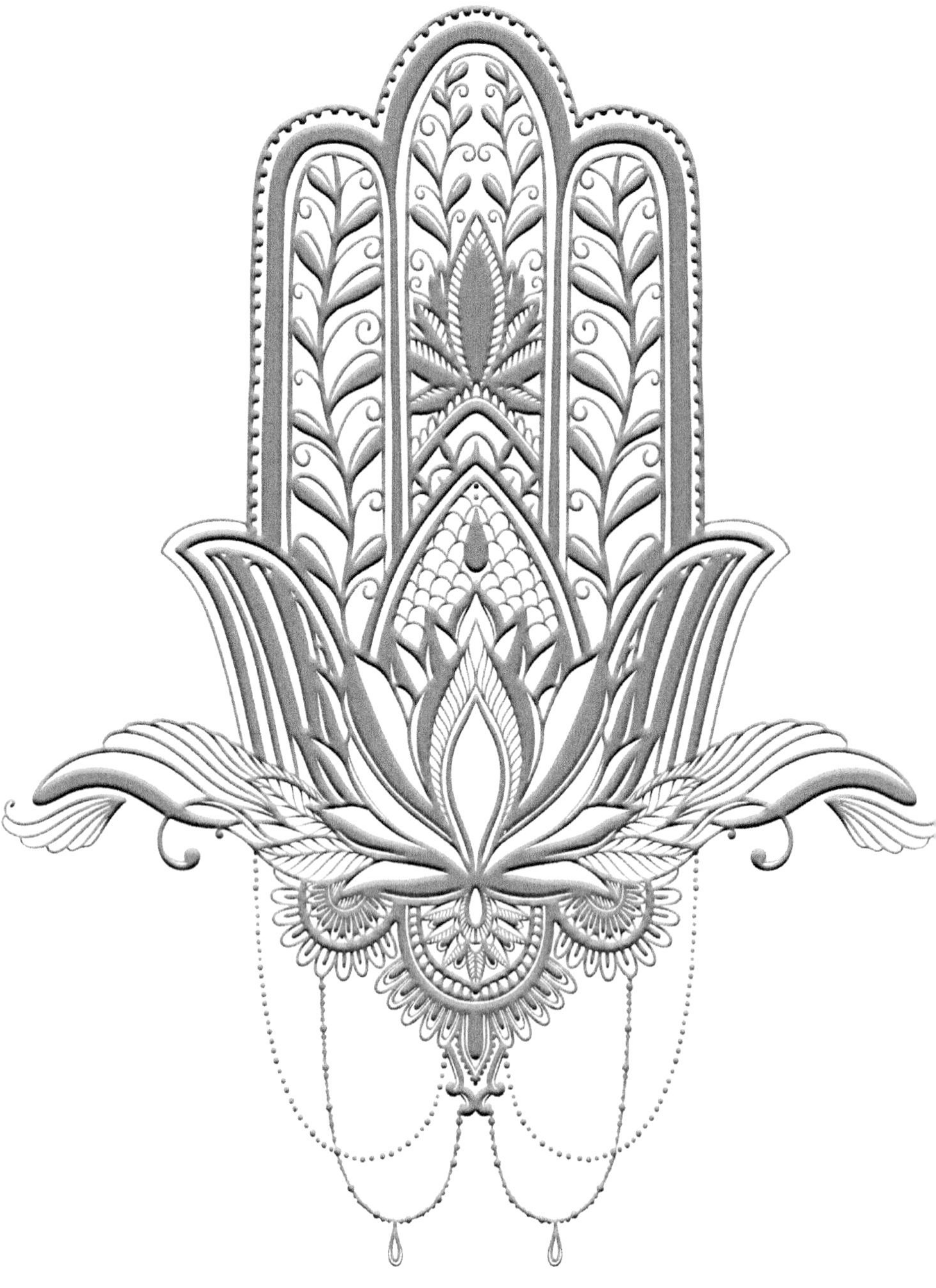

The Move to Hull

Hull was very different from Bradford—a lot less gray. Hull is on the East Coast of England and is known for its fishing industry. In my opinion, the best thing about Hull is its fish and chips. I like to joke that Hull is Hell—I didn't like Hull at all. I wasn't there long, just a year and a half before I left the country to marry, and I had very few friends. I didn't find the city interesting or special, but this could have something to do with my short stay. The people seemed to be so different from us. Bradford had so many Indians and Pakistanis, but Hull was full of English people, with very few Asians or people from anywhere else.

Our shop wasn't in an affluent area, but about a mile down the road, the area was "posh" and full of beautiful homes. People who lived on unemployment and welfare inhabited the area surrounding our shop. The customers exchanged vouchers for milk and other groceries. They talked differently than the people in Bradford too. Even within England, accents and dialects vary from one city to the next.

We moved to Hull after I graduated high school in 1985. I was sixteen and a half. In England, students graduate from school a lot earlier than they do in the United States.

"It's not necessary for you to go to college. You are getting married soon!" Mum exclaimed when she learned I had been accepted to attend Leeds Park Lane College after going to an admissions interview with one of my best friends. Attending the college meant I'd stay in Leeds or commute every day, and Mum was against me being away from home. I was really upset. I would have loved to go to college with my best friend. It would have given me the opportunity to escape home and seek freedom. However, it wasn't my destiny.

"He's been waiting to marry you since you were fourteen!" Mum yelled. "What's the point? You're just going to be a housewife!"

It was as if she thought it was acceptable to dictate what I was to become. I was meant to resign myself to it, even though it wasn't my choice at all. Events like this helped cement why my marriage was going to come at a big cost to me. My rights to education were taken away, and it looked like my future had been laid out for me.

My brother still wasn't very happy about his engagement. He told my mum he didn't want to go ahead with the impending marriage, but she didn't listen. They often shouted at each other about it.

"Look, I've told you so many times that I don't want this marriage! Why won't you listen to me! It's me who has to get married, not you! It's not fair!" Everything he said made complete sense to me, but my mum obviously refused to listen or care about what we thought.

"You will get married. Everyone gets married, eventually. You will realize I'm right one day; you just don't see it now," my mum said defensively.

Although we grew up in one country, the culture and traditions of our mother country kept us bound like prisoners and held us back from being like everyone else in the country we were born into. We were British and should have been allowed to be just like everyone else. Why were we being held to different standards and expectations that stemmed from a different country we had only visited once and from which we were far removed? Why weren't we living there instead if we were to follow those customs and traditions?

Mum wanted him to marry an Indian girl. Most Indian parents want their children to marry within their culture. We were supposed to marry other Indians, and they had to be from the same region we were from: the Punjab. They also had to be of the same religion—Sikh—and they had to be of the same caste. We belong to the *Jat* caste, which is the farmer caste, known to be landowners. It wouldn't be appropriate to marry someone from a lower caste, such as someone from the *Dalit* caste, who have been known to do the dirtiest jobs such as cleaning sewers, taking away the dead, etc., and unfortunately are also known as the "untouchables." It wouldn't be okay to marry someone from a higher caste either.

I don't care about any of this, nor would I be able to distinguish which caste someone is from; however, it was clear most Indians knew which caste other community members belonged to. The last name is tied to a particular region and distinguishes what they do: farmer, sweeper, goldsmith, etc. Therefore, if we are expected to marry within our caste and religion, it is unacceptable to marry someone who isn't Indian.

Much to my mother's disdain and pure disgust, Mandeep's girlfriends were English and white. She didn't approve of one girl and always said nasty things within earshot of us.

"That filthy girl just came into the shop again. I can't believe she has the nerve to step foot inside the premises. She has no self-respect. She's just trash!"

My brother and Stacy had a baby together, and the family kept it a secret. I only found out about the child after I had been forced into my marriage and later returned home to the shop.

I heard my mum and sister-in-law talking about Stacy in a very disparaging way.

"Did you see that tramp in the shop just a bit earlier?" asked my mum.

Davinder Kaur

"Oh, yes. I did see her. I wish I hadn't. Imagine having the nerve to set foot inside the premises! I wish we could just throw her straight out!" My sister-in-law released a sigh.

My mum looked at her and patted her hand in a soothing manner as if to say, "Fear not; I'm here with you. I'm on your side and always will be. I will always be against that tramp and will support you always."

I didn't know who this little boy was when he came into the shop. He was never pointed out to me; he was just kept a secret. I also didn't know who his mother was and had only heard her name mentioned. My little nephew came into the shop with his mum from the time he was a baby, and he didn't get to experience family love from any one of us. It breaks my heart. I feel guilty, but I wasn't aware of all the details. Once I found out, I know I failed to do the right thing and try to reach out to him. Fortunately, my brother maintained a relationship with his child and contributed to his upbringing.

Just before my dad passed away in 2008, my nephew was formally introduced to my family. My brother brought him to their house when he was sixteen or seventeen, and my parents finally accepted him. I believe my brother reached the point where he didn't care what Mum thought anymore. It was his life and his child, and he stood up for both of them. I'm proud my brother took that stance, even though it took him a long time to muster up the courage to do it.

My nephew is the most adorable human being. I met him for the first time when he came to San Diego in 2008, shortly after my youngest daughter was born. I'm sad about what happened to him. He was deprived of contact with our family because he was a different color and of different national origin. My nephew should have had everything my brother's other children had: the luxury of being accepted and not hidden away, shunned, ostracized, and ignored. He should have had the love of his grandparents on my brother's side and the love of his aunties, including myself. He should have been at birthdays, Christmas celebrations, and weddings.

The secrecy surrounding my nephew's existence reared its ugly head so many times in future circumstances. It was part of the deep character and intrinsic being of my parents, which stemmed from not only the way they had been brought up but the traditions and culture they had experienced and were a part of. It wasn't just secrecy; shame and honor were also strong factors. Nobody was to know of the deep secrets of the family, especially if these very secrets would cast us in a different light to other respectable families. That would bring shame and cause others to question the family's honor.

A "respectable" family had children who did everything the traditional way. They married someone chosen for them and only had children with that spouse and no one outside the marriage. If anything happened outside the norm, family members were required to maintain secrecy worthy of the Secret Service. We were not to divulge our secrets to anyone outside the immediate family, and, in many cases, we weren't comfortable enough to discuss it within our *own* family.

One example that comes to mind is when I visited England in 1997 after I had moved to America in 1991. It was shortly after my first daughter was born, but I'd already split up with her father and was going through a divorce. I was reminded by Mum not to speak about my divorce to anyone, including my grandma, and if anyone were to ask, I was to say my husband was working and couldn't travel with us. Mum didn't want me to shame the family because I had a child and was a single parent. I hated having to live such a lie, but this wasn't the first time I had to act. I'd already been told not to speak of family matters to anyone, including my running away and my divorce from Bik. My marriage to Bik had also been an act, as far as I was concerned.

Since we were reminded so often to remain secretive, it became indoctrinated into our psyche to some degree, kind of like a rule we couldn't and wouldn't break under any circumstance. My mum chose to share things that bothered her with her daughter-in-law. Since my sister-in-law lived in the same house, and my mum and her formed a very close friendship, it was understandable. She had to let her daughter-in-law know she was on her side and wasn't accepting of the situation my brother had brought upon them. Mandeep's wife was everything my mother had dreamt of in a daughter-in-law. She was pretty, hard-working, loyal, and dependable. She didn't complain, no matter what life threw at her. The circumstances surrounding her marriage with my brother weren't ideal, but she handled everything as the quintessential Indian woman is supposed to. My mother would do anything for this perfect daughter-in-law, who, in my mum's opinion, was a daughter in many ways and was more loyal and hard-working than we had ever been.

The Youth Training Scheme

I enrolled in a government-sponsored Youth Training Scheme—a one-year work/training program. The program helped recent high school graduates transition into work, and it was referred to as YTS for short. It functioned as a kind of apprenticeship or vocational training.

The secretarial program was facilitated by Pitman Secretarial College. I attended class for about a month and was placed in a job for a month or two. I was then required to return to class to learn more about typing, shorthand, composing business letters, and so forth. My first official work placement was with an accounting company in Cottingham, a pretty and very quaint village area of Hull. The job was okay, but my second placement at a travel agency was more profound and memorable.

My supervisor at the small, family-owned business was a quiet, middle-aged man who didn't say much, so it was surprising when he unexpectedly said, "You don't belong in an office; you need to be out there."

I wasn't sure what he meant, but his cryptic words have always stuck with me. Had he foreseen my future? I had discovered my love for travel while working at the agency. Nothing gives me as much joy as the ability to travel and experience new discoveries and adventures, which are even better the farther I get away from my home territory.

Perhaps he meant I was supposed to be in the public eye. Did that have anything to do with telling my story? I'm not sure. Honestly, I'm not a very confident public speaker; I get nervous in front of a room full of people. I did, however, discover I possessed a different kind of confidence at work: I was very strict.

Later, when I became a supervisor in San Diego, I grew accustomed to making decisions myself and didn't see the need to consult with my staff. This behavior was a direct result of my upbringing. I'd been told what to do, when to do it, and how to do it all my life. The very traits I hated had become part of me. My staff didn't take well to this type of supervision, and it helped me realize we are who we are because of our unique experiences. We must learn from our past, not hide from it. If we reflect on lessons learned, the past can provide many important answers about who we are today. Relationships, whether romantic or platonic, can become difficult if we don't educate others about our experiences and how they shaped our lives.

In a training class in San Diego, we discussed trust and the importance of earning it. I knew I had to let the class know how my upbringing affected the type of supervisor I had become. I told my classmates what had happened to me and how I came from a strict family. I talked about how I couldn't decide anything for myself, and how, at the age of fourteen, I was shown the picture of a boy I would later have to marry. Many were moved and shocked by my confession. Speaking my truth gave me a new sense of confidence and freedom, and I embraced it.

Developing My Own Independence

Toward the end of my time in the program, my personality began to develop more. I had discovered my autonomy and began to do things to shock my mum or make her very upset with me. I was saving my money and had already accumulated a nice balance from making the samosas when I was younger, so I began to use it for my own purposes. For example, I had worn glasses since I was seven, but I wanted to try contact lenses. I passed an eyecare shop every day, and I got an idea.

According to my mum, my appearance wasn't important until I got married; only my husband was to benefit from my looks. Looking back, I'm aware of the backward thoughts and traditions of my culture, but I didn't give it much thought when I was younger. I knew my mother wouldn't approve of what I wanted, so I made an appointment, attended the exam, and purchased the lenses without her permission.

I was faced with a new problem: It was impossible to cover up the fact I didn't need my glasses. I had worn them for many years because I was very near-sighted and practically blind.

My mum didn't realize anything different right away, but my sister did.

"You have lenses, don't you? I noticed you weren't wearing your glasses all the time, and I know you need to. It seemed strange to me, and now I can see why. You have lenses in your eyes! I can see them!" She stared at me with a very pleased-with-herself expression on her face. "I'm going to tell Mum."

"Don't! Please!" I pleaded, but it seemed like she enjoyed knowing I would get into trouble.

One day, my mum looked into my eyes and saw the lenses. She was furious about what I'd done without her permission.

"Who do you think you are, getting contact lenses without asking me? Is this what happens when you get the freedom to have a job and some money?"

"I'm really sorry, Mum. I knew you wouldn't let me have them, so that's why I didn't ask".

"*Churel*!" she shouted. *Churel* means witch.

She'd said it before, and I had heard it in movies. I wasn't too offended by the word itself; I was more upset knowing I was being sworn at or insulted.

"You are unbelievable! How could you? I'll teach you to go against my wishes behind my back." She extended her right arm all the way to the side of her body and slapped my face. She might as well have cut me with a knife—the sting of her hand against my flesh was sharp and painful.

"Ow!" I reeled in pain and fear and knew a second one was on the way.

She swung and connected again.

"Ow, ow, ow!" I cried.

She was mad and annoyed with me but eventually calmed down as though her actions had drained her of her emotions.

I believe buying the lenses behind my mum's back was just a sign of rebellion stemming from me realizing I had the right to choose what I wanted. This was just the beginning of a pattern of asserting my rights or making my own choices. We weren't permitted to make our own decisions, and we weren't supposed to focus on our appearance before marriage.

As time passed, I realized I absolutely did *not* want to marry the boy. Perhaps it was because the time was coming closer—after all, I was nearly eighteen—and it all began to sink in. I knew I couldn't marry a stranger; I didn't love him, and I wasn't attracted to him in the slightest. I sat in my room at night and thought about what I would do, and that's where I hatched a plan.

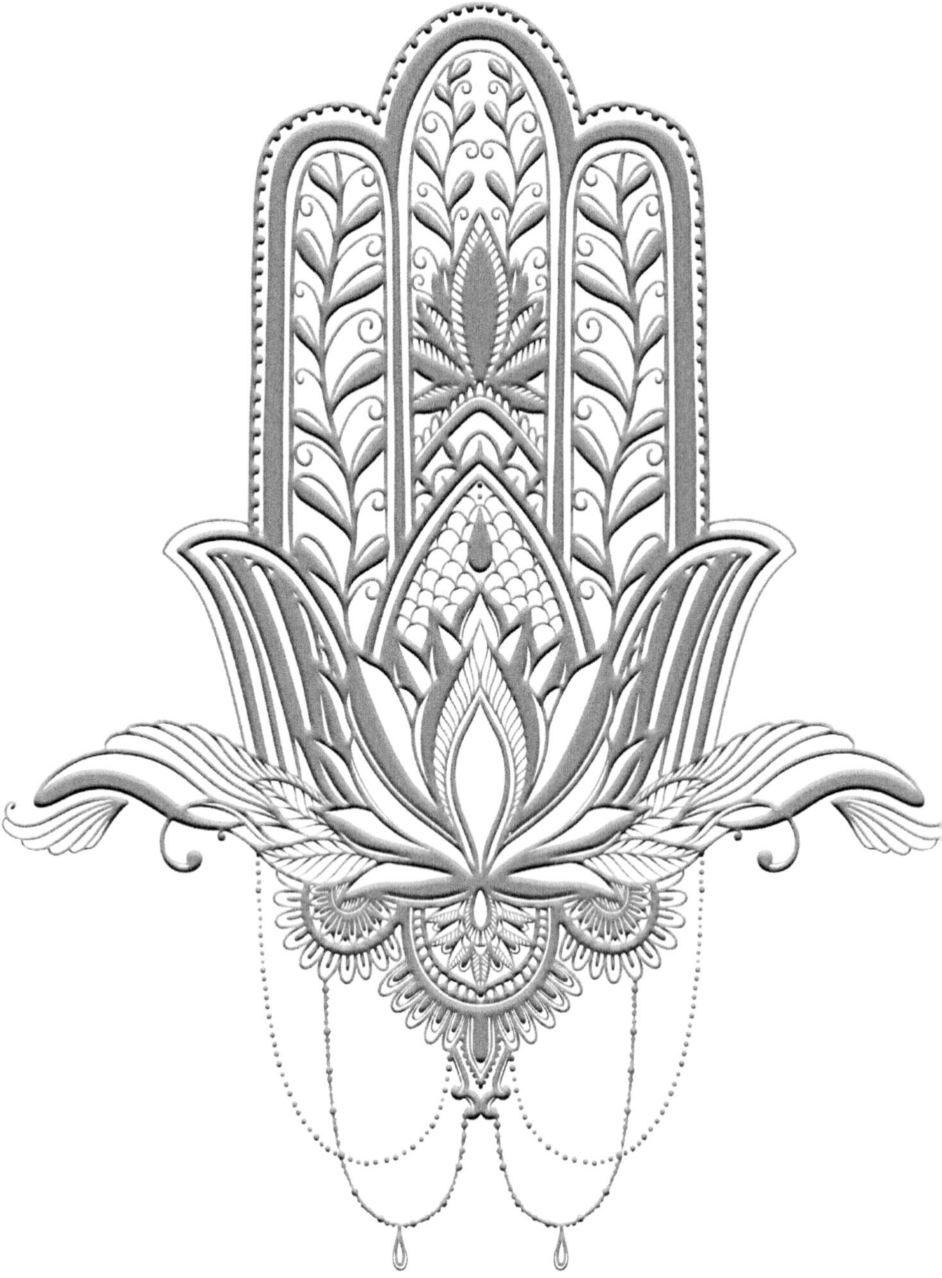

The Escape

I knew I had to pack a suitcase once I turned eighteen and get away as soon as I could. I'm not sure how I knew I shouldn't attempt this before I reached the age of adulthood, but some inner sense guided me to wait.

We now had a second shop closer to the city center in Hull, and I mostly went there on the weekends. I often ran the shop on my own, but my mum or dad joined me from time to time. My plan was to leave on a day Mum was there with me.

I clearly remember the day before I ran away. I'd just turned eighteen and had accumulated nearly £5,000 from the training program and my *samosas*. I was especially thankful to the man who was so impressed by my culinary skills that he hired me to make *samosas* for his business years earlier. Without him, I wouldn't have had such a nice bundle of savings.

I arranged for a taxi to pick me up at a certain time and explained I needed them to wait at the side of our shop. I had already bought a one-way ticket on a coach (bus) from Hull to London. I didn't know anyone in London, and I didn't know where I was going to stay. In fact, I had never been to London!

I called Mum to let her know I was on my way to the shop. Very uncharacteristically, she told me to take my time because it wasn't that busy. Once I arrived, Mum left for a short time and returned with a treat for me—a vanilla slice with custard in it. I figured she'd gone to visit her friend at one of the shops down the way and got it for me because she knew I liked them, and I'd just had my birthday. She was being so nice to me that I almost didn't feel like running away anymore, but I had to follow through with my plan.

When the taxi was scheduled to arrive the next day, I grew nervous. I had to get the suitcase down the stairs and somehow sneak it into the back room by the door, make it out to the back yard, and go through the side gate. I was so scared my dad would see me from the main shop, but I was able to make it outside with my suitcase and into the waiting taxi.

The taxi driver delivered me to the coach station in Hull, which was a short distance from our house. I paid the fare and got out of the car. My heart was beating fast, and I just wanted to get in the coach. Part of me wanted to turn around and go home. I wondered if my family knew I was gone yet, but they probably didn't. They were all busy. My brother and sister were helping my dad, and my mum was expecting me at the other shop.

I approached a few people to find out where the London bus was. My heart grew heavy as I boarded and found a seat, and my eyes filled with tears as I looked out the window. I felt small, alone, and vulnerable. Part of me wished I hadn't done it—that I was back home in my room—but I shrugged off that insecurity and reminded myself why I was leaving.

I worried my family had found out, or perhaps one of our customers had seen me get into the taxi and told my dad.

I worried I was being followed to London.

I worried the entire five-and-a-half-hour trip.

Arrival in London

I couldn't believe what I had done once I got off the coach at Victoria Station in central London. I had no clue where I was going to stay, but I knew I had to find an inexpensive hotel. Fear and apprehension settled into the pit of my stomach. I wanted the comfort of home.

If I could have been granted one wish, I wanted to close my eyes and undo everything I had just done. I walked away from the station, struggling a little with my suitcase and handbag along the way. People were everywhere, along with the traffic, red double-decker buses, and taxis. The city was bustling with activity. It was beautiful; I had never seen anything like it.

I passed some impressive hotels in Victoria, but I knew they were too expensive for me. The architecture was so different from anything I'd ever seen before; the buildings were amazing! People of all different colors and nationalities surrounded me, and I heard so many languages: French, German, Italian, and many more. It was like being in a different country. I couldn't believe I was still in England, and I wondered why we had never visited London as a family.

A taxi driver pulled over and opened his window. "Can I help you? You look a little lost. Can I take you anywhere in particular?"

"I'm looking for a cheap hotel. Do you know of any around here?"

"I know a good hotel near Warren Street tube station, not too far from Euston Square tube station and train station, about a five-minute drive from here. I've taken plenty of people there. It's really a bed and breakfast. If you want me to take you, just hop in."

"That would be great," I replied.

The driver took my suitcase and placed it in the boot (trunk), and I got into the taxi, relieved to be free of struggling with my luggage.

"I'm Jimmy, and I'm originally from Romania. I know this city well. I've been driving taxis for about five years now. What brings you to London?"

"Certain situations have caused me to be here. It's my first time visiting the city." I couldn't tell him why I'd run away to London. I didn't know him; I knew it wasn't advisable to talk to strangers or divulge too much information to them.

I stared out the windows at the passing scenery, enchanted by the sights and the busy city. It wasn't long before we reached the hotel, and Jimmy got out to help me inside, carrying the suitcase for me. He waited until I checked in and got my keys, and then he carried my suitcase up to my room. There was no elevator, and my room was two floors up, so I was grateful for his help.

"I will come back to check on you tomorrow," Jimmy promised.

I should have declined his offer, but I wasn't assertive enough and didn't have those skills back then. I only had manners, and my manners didn't allow me to respond negatively to someone, even a stranger.

I was puzzled by his statement but was eager to get into the room. "Okay, thank you so much, Jimmy."

I paid my fare and opened the door to my room. Once I got my bags inside, I dropped onto the bed to rest before heading out into the city. Surely, my family knew I was gone. Were they looking for me? I couldn't call home—I wouldn't. I'd made my decision and had to remain strong in my resolve. I finally got up and left to explore.

London was beautiful! It reminded me of *Oliver Twist* when Oliver had happier times after being adopted by the old gentleman.

There were gorgeous townhomes and a square named Fitzroy Square, which was close to the hotel.

I loved London then, and I love London now. It's been my favorite place for so many years, and I feel like I left a piece of my heart there all those years ago when I was just eighteen, when I was young and innocent. London is where I first discovered my freedom and happiness.

I walked around dazzled that first evening. I wanted to go back to Victoria Station because I felt a great connection to my arrival point. Instead, I explored Warren Street—it leads to the underground station I used quite a bit in the following weeks—and Fitzroy Square. I saw the Indian YMCA, which is a student hostel, the BT Tower in the distance, and some other buildings that looked mysterious and enchanting. People bustled around me in a hurry, and the distinct London cabs with plenty of space in the back for luggage moved up and down the streets.

I finally settled on a place to have dinner and indulged in a plate of pasta and a cup of tea. After my meal, I walked back to my hotel. I didn't feel lonely, but I thought about my family and what they were doing. I felt some guilt for whatever heartache I was causing them.

I wasn't sure what my plans were. Was I going to stay indefinitely, or would I have to get a job and move somewhere cheaper? I thought about this more and more over the next few days as I kept dipping into my purse. I would soon run out of money if I continued to stay at the hotel.

I went to the breakfast room in the basement early the next morning before going back out into the city. The tantalizing aromas of bacon and fresh bread wafted into the air, making me realize how hungry I was. I found a table and took a seat.

A few guests soon joined me, including Franz, a German man. He was tall and slender, with dark-brown hair and a moustache. He dressed nicely and wore a sweater over his shoulders with the sleeves around his neck. Although his accent was thick, he spoke

English well. He asked me about myself and why I was in London. I told him the whole story, and he was amazed.

"I'm glad you got away, Davinder. It's good you came here to London. It would have been awful if you had gone along with what your family wanted for you. I have heard of arranged marriages before, but I've never met someone who escaped one. From what I know, girls just go along with it, don't they?"

"They do, you're right. I just couldn't. It's not what I want for myself. I don't want to marry him."

"You're not going to, Davinder. You're safe here. You made a good choice to run away from all of that."

I felt so comforted by talking to him and confiding in him. Franz was easy to talk to, and I could see he was genuinely concerned. He and I got along well and often had breakfast together in the following weeks.

One morning, I saw Jimmy lingering outside as I left the hotel. Jimmy was a good-looking man. He was close to my height, perhaps an inch taller, and he had curly black hair. I found out later he was twenty-seven.

"Hi, Jimmy. How nice to see you again." I smiled as I approached him.

"How do you like the hotel?" He spoke with a deep foreign accent, but it sounded beautiful and was like music to my ears.

"It's really nice. Thank you for bringing me here. It's centrally located, and I love the area!"

"Can I take you out for dinner tonight?"

I was excited but extremely nervous. I said yes, nonetheless. I made plans to meet him outside the hotel that night. This was my first date ever! I'd never been out with a boy before, or been alone with one, or had dinner with one other than my brother or cousins. I tingled with excitement.

After confirming my date with Jimmy, I walked around London and purchased an underground tube pass. I loved it! I felt like I belonged. I took the tube to Victoria Station. The tube and train stations at Victoria are in the same building, so it's very busy with people heading to different destinations in central London and all over the country.

After I exited the tube, I walked to the coach station across the street to revisit my point of entry into London, and then I walked back to Victoria Station to thoroughly explore. It was an interesting place with many different shops and restaurants. I got a cup of tea and bought something to eat. I liked people watching.

Just before I headed back to meet Jimmy, I walked across Oxford Street and saw mothers and fathers with their young children. I was all alone and sad. I didn't have my family anymore. The Christmas lights were up already, and it was quite cold. I had never seen lights like the ones that adorned Oxford and Bond Streets. They were spectacular in their brilliance. The lights blinked, shimmered, changed color, and dazzled people with the magic of the season. I wished I was experiencing it with my family.

When I saw parents holding their children's hands, I felt the sharp pain of loneliness and the longing to have my family with me so they could see this amazing city and enjoy it too. However, I knew it was not meant to be, and I swallowed the deep taste of bitterness that had welled up in my mouth.

I rushed back to the Fitzroy Hotel to meet Jimmy on time. We had dinner at a nice Italian pizza restaurant. It wasn't too fancy, but it was cozy.

"How do you like this restaurant?" His accent was beautiful.

"It's lovely. I just love it. You chose well, Jimmy."

"I chose for you, my lovely. We can come here again, if you like." He gazed at me questioningly.

I looked at him, but I shifted my gaze because he was staring deep into my eyes. When I glanced at him again, he was still staring, and I giggled nervously. I wasn't sure what I was supposed to do. I had a nice time with him at the restaurant, though, and I didn't feel so alone.

"I'll let you know, Jimmy. Or perhaps we can try another place."

"As you wish. I will take you wherever you choose to go."

He continued staring, and I looked at him for only ten seconds or so before I glanced away again. We finished our dinner. I didn't want to drink any wine; I wasn't accustomed to drinking alcohol.

Jimmy dropped me off at the hotel after dinner and gave me a hug outside. He wrapped me in his arms and tried to kiss me, but I didn't let him. I wasn't supposed to make out with someone I wasn't married to. Jimmy wanted to see me again, but I didn't give him another chance because he was a little too intense. I felt a level of guilt, or maybe shame, because I wasn't supposed to associate with men. I'd never done that before, and I felt like I was doing something I wasn't supposed to do.

"Not right now, Jimmy."

"Why not? Just give in to your feelings. Have you ever kissed a man?"

"No." I shook my head.

"Allow me to be the first." He moved even closer to me, breathing over my neck and kissing me there. He tried again to put his mouth on mine, but I just wasn't ready.

"No, Jimmy, not right now. I'm not ready for this. I barely know you."

"You can get to know me. This is a great way to get to know me," he smirked and moved away. "Okay. Bye, Davinder. I will come by in a few days."

"Okay," I relented. I felt I owed him that much. He had already been a friend to me and had helped me find the hotel.

I walked back inside and went straight to my room. I sat on the bed and thought about the night's happenings and how my family would react if they knew I had been out to dinner with a man. I wondered how they'd feel about the almost-kiss.

Franz and I continued to meet for breakfast and occasionally went sightseeing together during my three-week stay at the hotel.

"We should really cut our costs and find a room somewhere else, don't you think? It's going to cost a lot if we carry on staying here."

"We will need *two* rooms," I clarified.

He nodded and laughed. "That's what I meant! I'm going to look at the evening paper. I'm sure we will be able to find something that works out cheaper for both of us."

I felt sad about leaving the hotel where I had stayed for several weeks. I have since been back twice. I stayed there when I visited London a few years after the first time. In 2014, I sought it out again and took many pictures. I told the manager about my fond memories from many years ago.

The manager was very happy to hear my story, and he allowed me to walk around and look at the room I had stayed in (it was empty) and visit the breakfast room in the basement.

An Indian couple owned the house Franz and I moved into in Paddington. I had my own room, his room was upstairs, and we shared a bathroom and had access to the kitchen. It wasn't long before he drew me in with a kiss and we became romantic. We hugged and kissed and went a bit further, but I didn't have sexual intercourse with him. I still believed I had to save myself for marriage. Franz was a gentleman—patient, understanding, and very respectful.

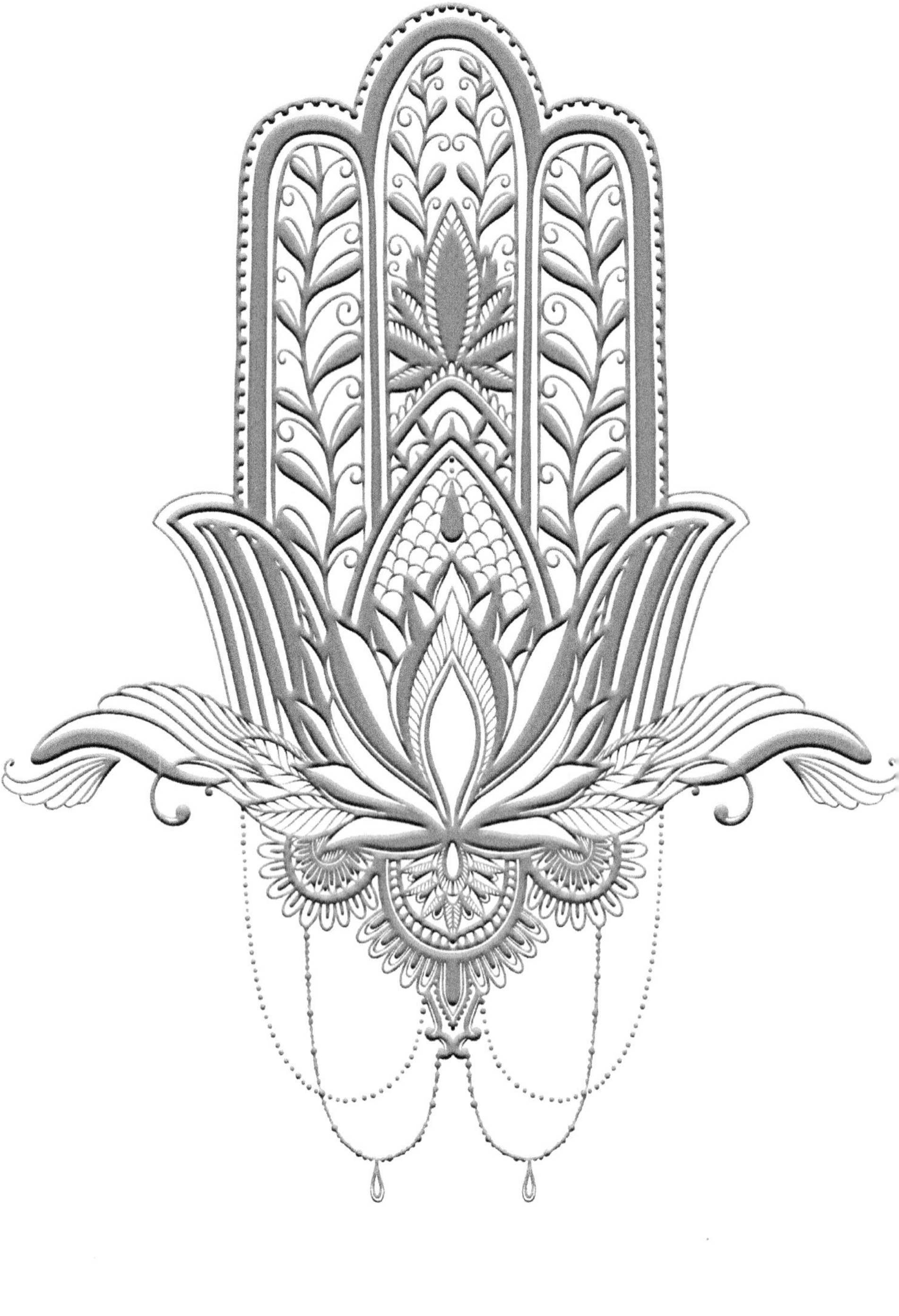

The Phone Call Home

I missed my family very much. I wanted to hear Mum's voice and let her know I was okay. The home in Paddington didn't have a phone, so I went looking for one. Making sure I had plenty of coins to deposit in case the call lasted longer than expected, I stepped into the phone booth. Business cards and advertisements covered the walls, and the stench of urine was overwhelming. It wasn't a pleasant place to be making a call from, but I had no choice.

So many questions flashed in my mind as I paused for a few minutes with a coin in my hand. I looked out at the blue sky.

What if nobody picked up?

What if they answered but didn't want to talk to me?

A lump formed in my throat, and my palms grew clammy. I held the coin tighter as I became more agitated about placing the call.

Finally, I deposited the required coins and dialed the number. The phone rang about five times before someone picked it up.

"Hello?" My mum's voice sent chills down my spine. It was so familiar, and she almost sounded sad.

"Hi, Mum, it's Davinder."

There was a pause, but I could feel the energy and anger palpating into the atmosphere and coming through the phone as though it would burn me with its heat.

"Why are you calling now?" Her tone was as icy as the London chill. "Why have you done this to me?" she demanded. "Do you know it's not just me you've done this to, but everyone, including Bik, his brother and his wife, and to your whole family? Why?"

"I don't want to get married, Mum, you know that."

"You are so selfish. How could you do this to us? I've been banging my head against the wall in your bedroom almost every night and crying so much. My teeth have gone crooked because of how much I've banged my head."

Mum was gaslighting me, but this was severe gaslighting. She attempted to make me feel guilty for causing her pain and suffering when, in reality, I was trying to get away from the pain and suffering *she* had forced upon *me*.

I was silent and listened to her yell.

"I won't ever forgive you for what you've done. Of all your siblings, I never would have believed that you would be the one to do this!" she shouted, shock filling her voice. "Are you coming home?"

"No, I'm not, Mum."

"Well, your grandma is really ill. She's not doing that well. Please come home," she pleaded.

I loved my grandma very much. Pain and weakness shot through me as tears ran down my face. I felt it was my fault, that I was the one who'd made her ill.

"I miss you all very much, but I can't come home. I will call again. Mum … Mum, you have to understa–"

She hung up on me. I barely managed to get the phone on the hook because I didn't have any strength left. I cried hysterically and didn't care if anyone heard me. I glanced outside to see if anyone was waiting to use the phone, but no one was, so I stayed a few minutes and cried until I finally calmed down.

All I could think of was my grandma as I stepped out of the booth. I got back to the house in Paddington and ran straight into Franz's arms. As sobs wracked my body, I tried to explain what had happened.

He held me close and stroked my hair. "Your grandma is going to be just fine. Don't worry. Everything is going to be okay, baby."

His strength made me feel much better. I don't know how I would have made it through that morning without him. He continued holding and consoling me as my tears drenched his shirt.

The next morning, I heard voices outside our building and thought they were asking about me. Paranoia took over my thoughts. I was convinced my mum had hired a detective, they had traced the call, and now they had come to take me away. I struggled with not wanting to be found, but I also wanted to know how my grandma was. I'd recently purchased a one-way ticket to Sri Lanka to visit Colombo, a popular destination at the time, but my plans were about to change.

Even though I didn't admit it to myself there and then, I knew I had to go home to see her. I knew I had to call home again and ended up making the call two days later. It didn't go well.

"Hello," my mum answered in a chillingly cold tone. "Your grandma is not doing well. You really should come home."

"Okay, Mum. I will," I cried.

Guilt rose within me, and I knew I wouldn't be able to forgive myself if anything happened to her.

"I will send your auntie to London to travel back with you. She will come tomorrow by train. We will see you when you get here".

I'm not sure why my auntie had to come to London. I was more than capable of traveling home on my own. I had to pack my belongings and had no idea how long I would be gone.

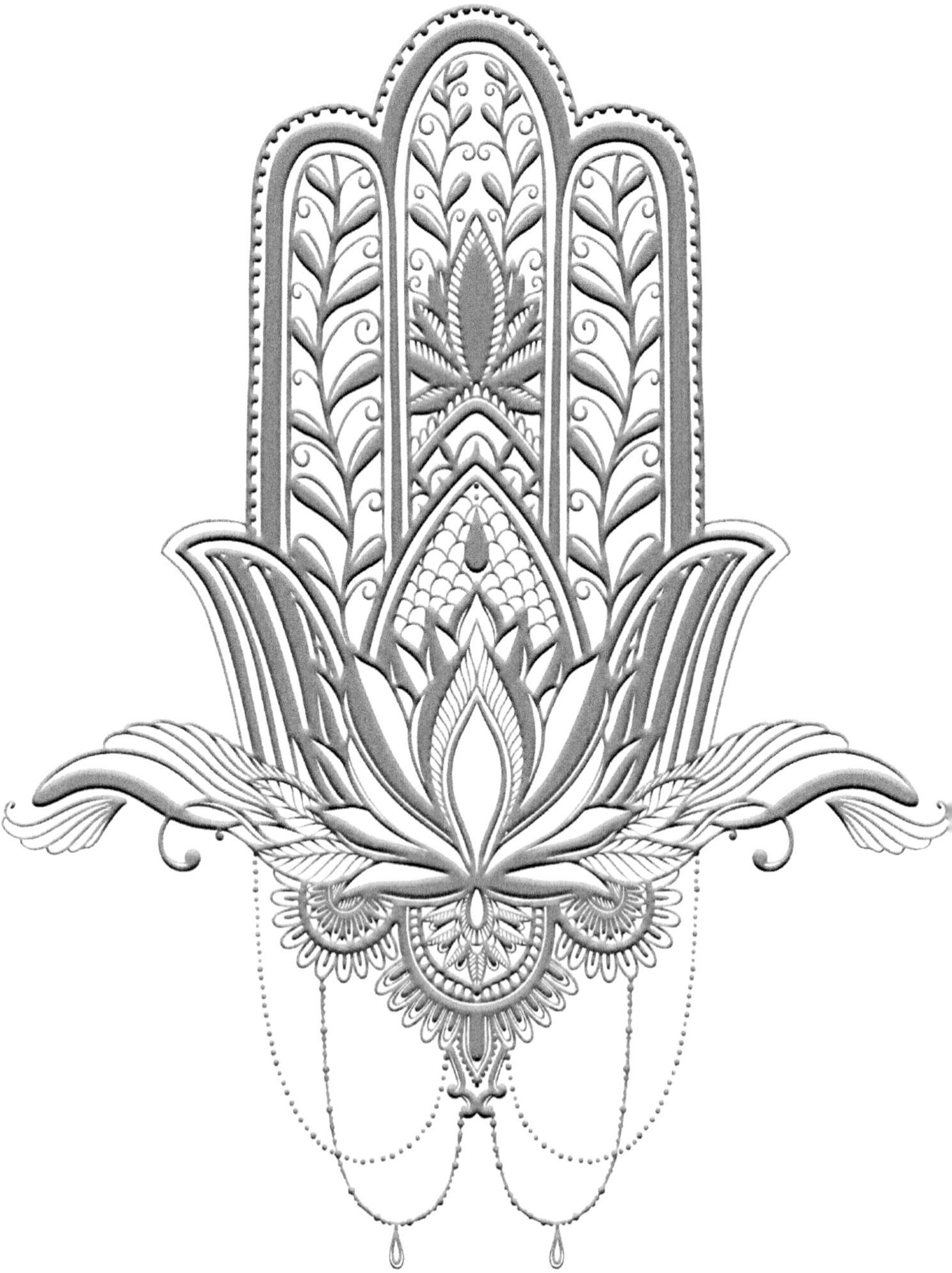

The Return to Hull

I had told Franz I was going home before my auntie arrived, and although he was a little upset, he understood. We had our last bittersweet hug just before my auntie showed up, and I wondered if I would ever see him again. We exchanged numbers and promised to keep in touch.

Sitting next to my auntie on the train, I closed my eyes and thought of everything that had happened. I felt almost dizzy with the realization I was going home, and I worried if everything would be okay. I thought of Franz, and then I thought of my grandma. It was just too much. I wanted to scream, "Why is this happening to me?!"

My mum picked us up at the train station when we finally arrived in Hull. She glanced at me briefly but didn't hug me. I had been ready to go to her, to give her a hug, but her rejection hung thick and heavy between us. It tore me up inside.

"Hello, Davinder. It's good that you are back," she said, greeting me with a disapproving tone. In the car, she ignored me and only talked to my auntie.

Once we got home, my dad greeted me with a smile. "Hello, Bindi. All right?"

It's noteworthy to mention that my dad and siblings hugged me. It wasn't long until the atmosphere was fraught with tension, courtesy of my mum shouting and flinging accusations at me.

"Look at what you've done to me." She pointed to her teeth. "I went into your bedroom every night. I would look and see that you weren't here, and it tore at my soul that you could do this to me, to all of us. You have put us through so much pain and misery. I banged my head on your wardrobe door; that's why my teeth are crooked now! It's all because of *you*!" she yelled. "How could you be so thoughtless?"

I felt incredibly sad and guilty. Again, my mum was gaslighting me to make me feel shame for her emotions. During her tirade, she told me no less than three times that she'd banged her head on my wall and wardrobe.

"I can't believe that, out of all my children, *you* would do this. I never expected this from you!" Mum scowled and glared at me in disdain.

"I'm really sorry, Mum. I'm sorry I upset you and that this happened to you. You shouldn't have done that. I'm really sorry."

Honestly, I doubted the story about her banging her head on the wall and her teeth being crooked. They didn't look different.

I went to stay with my grandma in Bradford and discovered she was perfectly fine. I had been deceived with a made-up story to get me to come home. My grandma didn't ask me too much about why I had left. I think she brought it up once but then left the topic alone.

One day, when *Bibi Ji* went out to go to the store, I made a call to Germany.

"Hello?"

"Hi, Franz, it's Davinder. How are you?"

"I'm doing better now that you've called," he replied excitedly. "I really miss you. How is everything going?"

"I'm sorry to do this to you, but would it be possible for you to call me back? I'm calling from my grandma's phone."

"Sure thing."

I hung up the phone and it rang a few moments later.

"Hello, Davinder," he said warmly and with concern.

The truth is, I never really fell in love with Franz. He was nice, but it wasn't like it was supposed to be, not like the romance stories I had read. I don't know how I knew it, but I had read enough novels that I knew exactly how I was supposed to feel. He wasn't "the one."

"How's your grandma?"

"Oh my gosh, Franz! You wouldn't believe it! I was tricked into coming home. Nothing was wrong with my grandma. She was perfectly well. They *tricked* me! Can you believe that?" I cried incredulously.

"No way! You're kidding! I'm completely shocked. Amazed, even."

At this point, it wasn't apparent what would happen upon my return to Hull. I was uncertain if I would be pushed back into the marriage I'd attempted to escape.

"I want to go back to London. I wish you were there, but I don't think I'm going to be able to go again," I said defeatedly.

"Davinder, I wish I were in London too. I miss it, and I miss you. It's not the same being here in Germany, but I have to get back to work now. I've had a lot of time away. Why don't you try to come visit me?"

"I won't be able to go anywhere right now. They watch me closely. I think they're afraid I might run off again. I'm really surprised my grandma left me all alone today." I sighed. "Listen, I need to go before she gets back. I miss you. I'll talk to you soon, okay?"

"Okay, Davinder. You take care and call me soon. I miss you."

We ended the call, and I felt sad, dejected, and miserable.

I got into trouble when my grandma found the call on her telephone bill. One of my aunties lived in Germany, but my grandma knew it wasn't her number. My grandma was on a fixed budget. I felt bad, but I hadn't been on the outgoing call that long. She told my mum, and I admitted to the call when my mum questioned me. Luckily, they didn't ask too many questions, but they were very disapproving and disappointed with me again.

I stayed with *Bibi Ji* in Bradford for a week or two before returning to Hull. My mother often tried to ask me why I had run away, even though she knew why. The argument that followed started the same way each time.

"I don't want to get married."

"You can't do this. The boy has been waiting to marry you since you were fourteen. How can you do this to him? His brother and sister-in-law have been waiting too. Everyone wants this marriage, so how am I supposed to tell them it's not going to happen?"

I was very sad and upset to hear everything she said.

"I can never think about you the same way after what you've done to me and the family."

I felt pressured and wanted to get away again. It was as though the walls were caving in on me and I was about to be crushed. I wished I hadn't come back from London.

My mother's gaslighting worked, as it usually did, and I finally gave in. "Yes, I will marry him."

In the back of my mind, I thought I would be able to get away from them and finally have the freedom to leave the man I was going to marry because they wouldn't be around. I planned to leave him shortly after the marriage. It would be easier to make another getaway when I was in another country, and they wouldn't be able to stop me. I was going to give in to what they so desperately wanted—my marriage—but I would get away from it, eventually. I had no clue what I was getting into. I shouldn't have agreed to something I didn't want.

According to the United Kingdom government, marriage is between two people who love each other. Forced and arranged marriages allowed the arriving person a ticket to stay in the country. People got married and, in many cases, left the spouse as soon as they received permanency. I had read newspaper articles about this kind of trickery and abuse.

I didn't connect any of that to my situation; it seemed like a completely different set of problems. Mr. Shergill knew Immigration was cracking down on those who cheated the system. He also knew it would be difficult for the boy to re-enter England, so his next-best plan was Denmark.

We were to live with his daughter and her husband and young child for a few weeks until the wedding and then move into our own place. Mr. Shergill was a smart man and knew it was more likely to be approved if the boy applied for a tourist visa to Denmark. He hadn't visited before and could say he wanted to see Denmark and other European countries. Sadly, I didn't connect the dots until later. They used my citizenship so the boy would gain entry into Europe and, eventually, England.

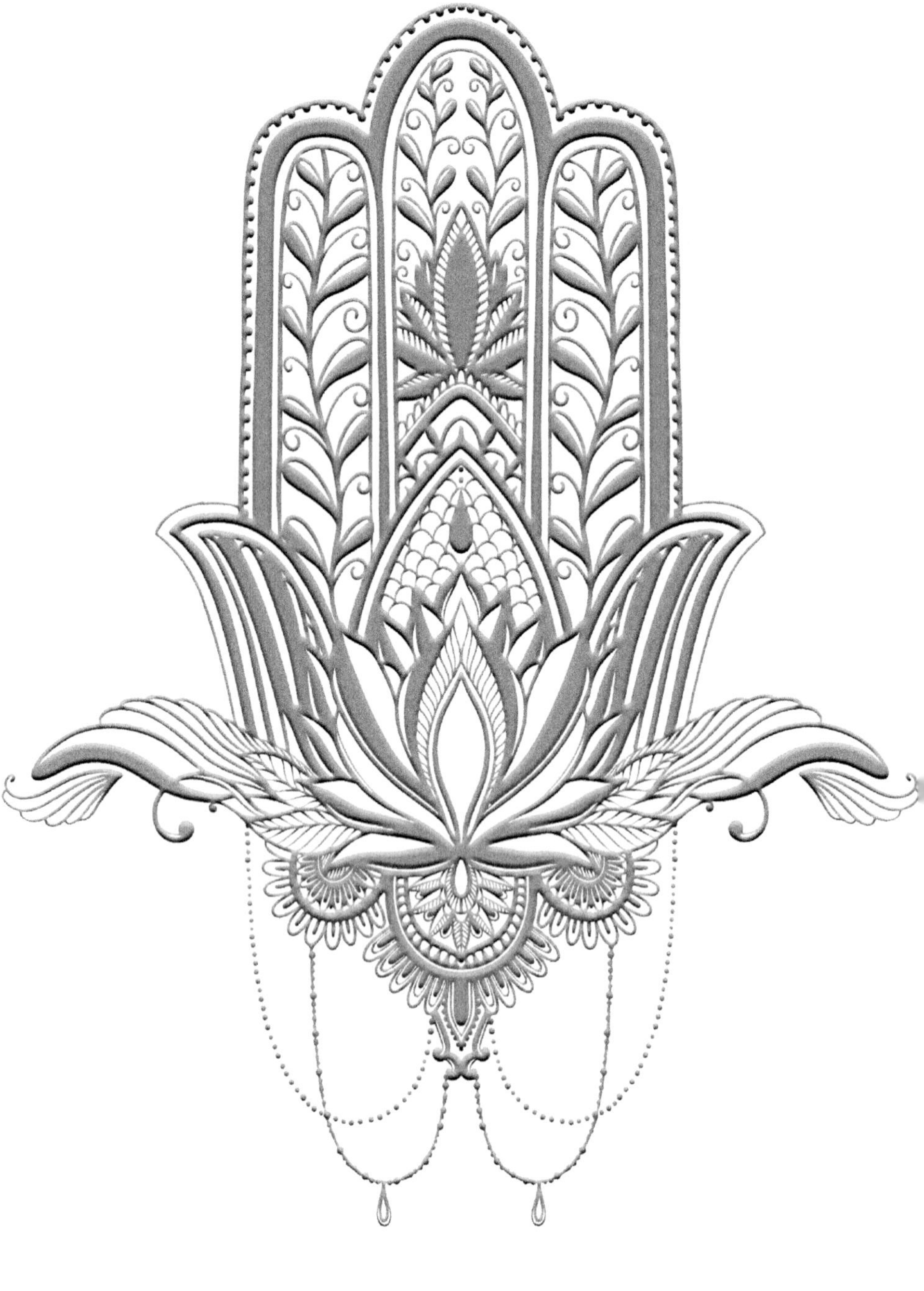

Hello, Denmark!

"Don't speak to the family we are going to stay with about your running away or not wanting to get married. They don't need to know. I've lost my trust in you and can never forgive what you did," my mum said on the flight to Denmark, her face twisted in anger and frustration.

Her words and stern tone left no doubt I had disappointed her in a very big way.

I felt guilty for what I had done. She should have been happy with the impending marriage of her daughter—something she had planned years ago.

"I won't, Mum."

It had snowed and was bitterly cold when we arrived in Denmark in March of 1987. We were at least three weeks early; the wedding wasn't until April 5th.

Mr. Shergill collected us at the Copenhagen airport and drove us to Ishoj. The trip didn't take long, and the town wasn't very remarkable. It certainly wasn't as special as London and didn't interest me at all. It was more modern than Hull or Bradford, but I didn't particularly like it.

Mr. Shergill took us to the Little Mermaid statue by the water in Copenhagen. I still have a picture of me standing in front of it. Compared to Ishoj, I thought Copenhagen was much prettier with its colorful buildings. There was a lot to see, including the popular Nyhavn area where there are many shops, restaurants, and cafés overlooking the harbor. We visited Tivoli on Vesterbrogade, the main street that leads to Nyhavn. Stroget, a main shopping avenue, had some of the best ice cream. It was impossible to avoid the delicious aroma of freshly baked waffle cones. Once I smelled it, I had to have one. Waffles were served with our choice of ice cream flavor, a dollop of whipped cream, and topped with a cherry. Delicious!

After Mr. Shergill showed us around, he took me to apply for a work visa. I was confused and didn't understand why I needed one. No one told me anything. I had no idea how long I had to stay, why I had to work, and why I had to remain in the country. I wasn't considered important enough to know details.

I decided to ask Mr. Shergill, even though I probably wasn't supposed to ask him any questions—like a good obedient girl. However, I was very curious as to why I needed a work visa. I thought I was there to be married, so why did I have to work?

"Mr. Shergill, why do I need a work visa? I'm British and can travel anywhere within Europe without a visa. Why do I need permission to work here?"

"Davinder, if you are going to stay here longer than three months, you need to have a visa to work. The government needs to know you are independent and capable of supporting yourself. So many people could claim poverty and file for benefits. This way, if the government sees you are working, they won't be suspicious of your intentions. Besides, you might be here longer than three months. Bik might not be able to get to England straight away. You will need to save money to pay for your own accommodation. Of course, you are welcome to stay with my daughter and her family, but you might be more comfortable in your own place after the wedding."

This made sense to me. I was grateful for the explanation, even though I resented that I had to stay in a strange place for an unknown period of time with the boy they wanted me to marry. Still, I couldn't say anything about this now as my mum had already forbidden me to talk about running away and not wanting to get married.

I completed the paperwork and received a number similar to the National Health Insurance number in the United Kingdom and the Social Security number in the United States. We also applied for my marriage registration ceremony—the ceremony that made my traditional, foreign wedding legal in Denmark.

I've blocked out a lot of this period, especially the times immediately before, during, and after the wedding. I know my mother only stayed with me for a few days before returning home. Mr. Shergill also went back to England and left me with his daughter and her husband. They were nice, but their apartment was just another home away from home for me.

Mr. Shergill's daughter followed the Punjabi customs to the letter. She was a prime example of a woman who did what she was supposed to do: have an arranged wedding, make it work, have children, and cater to her husband's needs, as well as those of guests and family. Although she spoke English well and I knew her father from Bradford, I have strong doubts she was native to my home country. I suspect she was born in India and immigrated to England before moving to Denmark. The fact Mr. Shergill was very strict and influential likely played a large part in how she lived her life.

Before the wedding, the boy arrived to stay at the *same* apartment. In our culture, couples don't live together before marriage, so this was very bizarre. Again, I wasn't informed of anything. My feelings were irrelevant. I was just a character in the plot.

We stayed under the same roof for about two weeks without exchanging so much as a word, except for perhaps a greeting on the first day he arrived, and then we were pretty much kept apart or monitored. I had my own room, and he shared with the little boy. Mr. Shergill's daughter gave me instructions on the first evening the boy arrived.

"When you need to go to the bathroom, just let me know. I will make sure the path is clear and the bathroom is empty. I must be certain he's not in the living room or somewhere nearby when you have to walk in." She paused and looked at me. "Do you have any questions about this, Davinder?"

"No." I shook my head. She had been clear, but nonetheless, I found it very strange. I felt like this was something happening on television and not to me. It was too much to comprehend.

"Just come and find me. I'll be in my bedroom or the kitchen. If I'm in the bedroom, just knock on my door. When he needs to go, he's going to do the same and my husband will make sure the path is clear for him. Is that clear, or do you have any questions?" She'd asked the same question twice in about two minutes, and that was a bit comical.

"No, I'm okay with that. I'll come and find you," I told her. It all sounded so strange.

What was even more peculiar was that I had to be in the kitchen and make the food along with the daughter, and then help her serve the food to him and her husband. I went right in front of them to serve the food and avoided eye contact with Bik. I basically said nothing to him, and they kept us separated from each other in the apartment. As if we wanted to get together, anyway! At least, *I* didn't. I would have run, given the chance, but I wasn't thinking of doing it again until after the marriage. I would tell him I wanted a divorce soon after the marriage.

I didn't have that much interaction with Mr. Shergill's son-in-law. He seemed nice enough, and he also wore a turban, just like his father-in-law. It was clear this Punjabi family was more traditional than mine. I do, however, recall they ate meat, as I had helped Mr. Shergill's daughter make chicken curries, other vegetarian dishes, and roti.

Their little boy had a *joora*, which meant his hair was uncut and gathered in a bun on top of his head. Young boys wear their hair in a *joora*, but they switch to wearing a turban when they become young men. Devout Sikhs don't eat any meat, smoke or drink, so it was obvious their family was strict but not completely devout. Thinking about the first few weeks I lived under the same roof as the boy, it strikes me that this is so far removed from how I envisioned a relationship with the man I married. In my romance books, the stranger and the heroine shared a glance or some other small interaction that set everything in motion. They had discussions and encounters—some of them romantic and some of them not romantic. Emotions ran high until she realized the man tormented her soul so much that she couldn't stop thinking about him. After a span of time, she ended up falling in love with him.

I know the books I read are fiction, but I also believe the stories in those novels hold little nuggets of truth when it comes to relationships. I also am realistic in knowing true love might not be how it is in the books and on television.

There was absolutely no romance leading up to my marriage. The boy and I had encounters that involved no contact, no looking, and no emotions other than my dread and resignation at having to do this against my will just to make others happy. I was quite subdued in those weeks leading up to the marriage. On the other hand, I heard him laugh and joke with Mr. Shergill's son-in-law. It was obvious Bik was in high spirits and certainly wasn't miserable.

My family arrived in Denmark a few days before the wedding. Our shop remained open, so my siblings stayed home to help at the store, but my parents, grandma, uncles, and aunties flew over. The apartment wasn't big enough to accommodate everyone, so some of them were put up at the host family's friends' homes. My parents and grandma stayed in the apartment.

I'm not certain I knew the date of the wedding until later. I just had to be there. Nervousness built up inside me as everyone arrived and the marriage moved forward. I tried to numb myself and block out what was happening. It was the only way I could cope with it.

Punjabi wedding celebrations last two to three days. The evening before my ceremony, all the women and girls performed *giddha*, a traditional Punjabi dance involving clapping and singing. We had a ceremony where *mehndi* (henna) was applied to the hands of nearly all the girls and women, and first and foremost, to me.

The bride receives the best *mehndi* design. The color shows up richly if it is applied a day or two before the ceremony. The longer the *mehndi* is left on the hands before it's washed off, the better. However, it needs to be washed off eventually, as it will become dry and start falling off and causing a mess. The *mehndi* application ceremony is a way of wishing the bride good health and prosperity as she embarks on her new journey.

After my ceremony, we enjoyed samosas, Indian sweets, and *chai*. The girls looked at each other's *mehndi*, remarking how beautiful it looked, and they gossiped and giggled. Someone applied red nail color to my fingernails and toenails. At one point, I heard someone say the boy wasn't handsome enough for the girl, but it didn't make me feel any better. No one bothered to notice I wasn't excited or happy—they didn't seem to care. They were having fun and that's all that mattered.

Forced Marriage Day

The apartment bustled with activity the day of the ceremony. I had to go through the traditions of the Indian wedding, including a Punjabi bathing ritual called the *chura* in which the bride-to-be's maternal uncle puts ivory and red bangles on her. I was terrified of this ritual because I thought my uncle had to be in the bathroom while I was bathed, but I was modestly dressed when he put the bangles on me. This was such a relief, as nothing was explained properly to me. I couldn't ask or didn't feel comfortable enough to ask.

I don't really remember much about the wedding ceremony, but in a traditional Punjabi wedding, the bride wears a lot of red and gold and has her head covered with her *dupatta* (also known as *chunni*). This is the first time, in many cases, she gets to apply makeup. The groom traditionally wears a regular business suit or a traditional Indian *kurta-pajama*, a trouser-like garment with a long top. The groom usually wears a turban. It can be any color, but it's usually a nice bright red or pink. The bride and groom typically sit on a stage or at the very front, closest to the priest. The priest reads from the *Guru Grant Sahib*—the holy Sikh bible. At a certain part of the service, the couple rises to do the *phere*. This is where the bride follows the groom around the perimeter of the stage a set number of times—usually four. The ends of their *dupattas*, which consist of the *chunni* and some of the cloth from the turban, are usually tied together in a knot, symbolizing togetherness.

I can't remember exactly what I wore on my wedding day. I know I was dressed in red with gold threading, but I can't recall if I wore a traditional red Punjabi outfit called a *salwaar/chameez*, which is a pair of loose, baggy pants with a long dress over it, or if I wore a red *sari* or a long dress over tight pants. I know I wore a lot of gold jewelry and makeup for the first time. Again, I have blotted out the details, as I never wanted to think back to that day.

After the service, I had to sign documents at the temple. The thought never crossed my mind not to do so, as my plan all along was to just file for divorce as soon as I could. I now realize this was another opportunity for me to escape this event, but this would not have been the right time to draw attention to my desire not to go ahead with the marriage. It would have further embarrassed my family. It was simply easier to stick to the plan to escape after everything took place and they were all gone.

Everyone gathered in a big hall that had been booked for the reception party. There was a lot of food, beer, wine, and other alcohol, as well as *chai* and Indian sweets. Our guests rejoiced in the occasion with food and dancing. Afterward, the guests were given a box of sweets to take home.

I have some flashbacks to the time after the ceremony. I remember Bik dancing, but I'm certain I would have refused to dance. I know everyone was happy, and I was the only one who wasn't. I really thought I was supposed to be happiest on this day. From what I knew, people who get married were supposed to be excited and anticipating every single minute of their big day. Well, I didn't feel the same way. I went through the motions and did what was requested of me.

Inevitably, I thought back to Princess Diana's wedding. She was still married to Prince Charles in 1987, and to me, her fairytale wedding was the best vision I had of a happy wedding day. It was one I would have loved to have experienced in just the same way. However, I didn't even know this stranger. I had barely spoken ten words to him, and I wasn't willing to speak to him.

Perhaps everyone didn't care, or maybe they were so happy themselves that they couldn't notice I was miserable. I'm not sure. I believe, in my culture, it wasn't important whether the girl was happy or excited. It was a duty or obligation, and therefore, it wasn't a major concern as to whether I was happy or not. My feelings were irrelevant.

Most South Asians think two people will get closer and develop a bond over time in an arranged marriage. My family knew mine wasn't a love marriage. They were aware I wasn't ecstatic and eager to get married, and they knew I didn't know him and had no romance with him. In fact, romance was frowned upon.

This happened to nearly every South Asian girl (Punjabi girls, at least) at that time and was nothing unusual. Still, it wasn't easy for me to accept, as I knew the life I wanted for myself. I didn't ascribe to the same expectations the Indian community and my family had of me. I hadn't grown up in India; I wasn't Easternized, but none of that mattered to any of them.

The evening of the wedding resulted in us being alone together in a room for the first time in the same apartment where we had stayed. I remember feeling nothing special about him. He was just an average-looking young man who was a few years older than me. I remember the way he laughed annoyed me, and I didn't like his smile. I'm not sure why, but he bugged me straight away. He only spoke Punjabi, and I resented having to use the language I wasn't accustomed to speaking. I had no special feeling of wanting to be with him, but I had a deep, horrible knowledge of what was expected of me now that I was his wife.

We were told where we were to sleep. When it was time to go to bed, we went to that room and did what everyone expected of us.

"Davinder," he said in his deep Punjabi accent, "now that we are married, we need to be together. Have you ever done it with anyone else?"

"No, I haven't."

"You're my wife now, and I've been waiting for you. I've been looking forward to this day and to our marriage."

I wanted to say I hadn't looked forward to it at all, that I didn't want to be there and married to him. I couldn't say the words, though, as I feared my mum and others were listening outside the door. I had seen Bollywood movies where this often occurred on wedding nights. The bride and groom had an audience outside their door, with eager eavesdroppers listening to what was going on in the room. I felt this was very perverse and invasive. I couldn't have this conversation with him yet; it would have to wait. He moved toward me, and I cringed deep inside. Unfortunately, I did what I had to do.

I had grown up with the belief I was supposed to wait until marriage for my first intimate encounter. I was now married, and I allowed it to happen. I knew it was expected, but when I think back now, I should have declined. I shouldn't have even gone ahead with the marriage. Even though I knew I was going to get divorced, I think it would have been so much more of a struggle if everyone had found out I hadn't given in. However, because I was submissive, I didn't raise any suspicions; I did what was expected of me. It was incredibly horrible that I had to sleep with a stranger. I didn't have feelings for him and hadn't been romanced by him, yet we were expected to be intimate because we were married. I remember how he questioned my purity the next day.

"Davinder, there's no blood on the sheets. Did you know that there's supposed to be blood?"

"I don't know why there isn't. I have no idea."

He stared at the sheets again and muttered something.

"What did you say, Bik?"

"Oh, nothing. I'm thinking that perhaps there doesn't always have to be blood. After all, you said you hadn't done it before, right?"

"That's correct. I haven't."

He must have thought I didn't save myself for marriage (which is not the truth). I felt so betrayed. I did what I was told and did it the right way, but he was still suspicious of my virginity. I was angry that he didn't believe me. It wasn't fair that he questioned my integrity, especially when I had done my best to live by certain ethical codes and standards.

I didn't think much of him. He was a willing participant in the marriage, and I felt like he was the perpetrator. I was angry that I had to marry him because he wanted to be married to me. I knew it was mainly the fault of his parents and the matchmaker, but he also wanted this marriage, and I certainly didn't want him.

I had gone through the motions with him, and it wasn't special or something I cared to remember. I felt obligated and pressured to give in to expectations. I understood my culture and what was expected of a wife. When he showed his character by the very words of doubt he spoke, I found him even more distasteful.

Mum asked if we had "done it" when we left the room, and I said we had. She was standing with the daughter-in-law and a few other women. They chuckled and acted like it was a joke or something. When I look back upon this situation, I can't believe they were concerned about sex. However, it's obvious they needed to know the marriage had been consummated properly.

That same day, we had our registry wedding in Ishoj. The first wedding had been our Indian wedding, but we now had to be officially recognized by the Danish government, and that is why we had to have the registry wedding.

After the registry ceremony, and when we were back in the apartment, Mum approached me.

"Do you want to go on honeymoon, Davinder?"

"Yes, I would love to go somewhere."

I knew most people went on honeymoons, and I wanted to go on one too. After all, I had been forced to marry, so I might as well complete the package. I also wanted to get away from all of them.

Ideally, it would have been great to get away from Bik, but I knew it wasn't possible.

"Can I go to Italy?"

"Sure. Where in Italy?"

"I'd like to go to Venice and Rome, if possible. How long can we go for?"

"You can go for a week. I'll call a travel agent and get it booked for you to leave within the next few days."

I hadn't been there before, but as of today, I have been there at least six times. I really love Italy. I'm glad I didn't let my ordeal put me off. For the remainder of the day, my mum helped me look at some apartments where my husband and I were to move into as soon as we came back from our one-week honeymoon. Since the apartments in Copenhagen were expensive, we settled on a studio apartment, which was in Frederiksberg. It was on the top floor of an old building. There were no elevators, and the bathroom was down the hall. The bathroom only had a toilet and a sink. There was no shower. If we wanted to have a bath or shower, we had to go to the public bathhouse. This was so bizarre, but I really had no choice. The price was reasonable, and the location was very good.

The "Honeymoon"

Venice was one of the most beautiful places I'd ever visited, and I was sad I had to experience it the first time with a stranger. I wanted to be with someone who could make it special. It was odd to be forced to continue the charade of the happy couple on their honeymoon. Honeymoons are for people who love each other, not complete strangers.

Who were we fooling? I didn't want to fool anyone, but it's exactly what we did—we fooled everyone around us. I felt like I was trapped in a sick, sadistic experiment and wouldn't wish it on my worst enemy. It's true that some people didn't suspect I was on my honeymoon, but what about those who saw us and automatically thought we were a newly married couple or boyfriend and girlfriend?

No one could possibly imagine I had been married under duress. Even though I was eighteen and understood what a marriage was, I can't say I was properly aware of what it involved and what that might mean to me long term.

I was conflicted with my culture dictating I had to be with someone I didn't care about, whereas my heart really wanted more for me. It wanted the love and romance akin to what I'd read in my books. However, I read romance, not horror, and I was going through horror at the time. I hated having to be with someone and hang out with him every minute of the day, when we had nothing in common. Yet I had said yes because I had no choice and wasn't allowed to use my voice to express my opinions.

Mum had constantly reminded me he had waited for me for four years, as had his family. It seemed everyone had waited for this marriage. The cruel reality of it was, I had said yes when I was a child, but now I was bound to the agreement because of pressure and expectations.

In my culture, we were expected to go along with what our parents wanted, and we didn't argue. I had tried to object and make my voice heard, but they didn't want to listen. I feared some type of punishment if I didn't go through with it.

I had heard stories of girls being disowned—or worse. Some girls were attacked or killed as part of an "honor killing" if they said "no" to marriage. The family considered their honor and reputation much more important than what their child wanted. Honor killings should be called dishonorable killings, as they certainly aren't honorable. They are given this name to show a family views their honor above anything else. They would do anything to protect the family name and spare themselves being shamed in the community. I had read about them in the newspapers, and even though I don't think my family would have done that to me, I gave in to the pressure, the guilt, and the marriage they so desperately wanted for me.

Our hotel in Italy wasn't very remarkable, but I didn't intend to spend much time in the room, anyway. I found it very strange that our room had two single beds. Obviously, they didn't know we were on our honeymoon, and I didn't want to correct them.

"Bik, you take this bed. I will take the other. I don't think it's a good idea for us to sleep together again, and it was wrong to do so on our wedding night. We need to get to know each other before that happens again."

We should've had the same conversation on our wedding night. Did I feel more confident now that I was away from family and friends and we were in another country?

Bik didn't seem too happy, but I knew I made sense and had brought up a valid point. He finally agreed, and we weren't intimate during our honeymoon.

I knew instinctively that Bik wanted the marriage. I had known from the very start, all the way back to the phone calls. Mum had always said he was eager to speak to me, but he had mentioned he was very happy to talk to me. I also knew it from the wedding night by how he had no problem when it came to consummating the marriage. If he had hesitated, I certainly would have welcomed it! However, he had wanted the whole package, as far as I know. He brought honor to his family by giving them what they wanted because it's what *he* wanted too.

We stayed in Venice for three days and went to Rome for four. Venice was just as I'd seen in the magazines. We visited St. Mark's Square and saw many beautiful buildings, churches, and magnificent art. We took in the scents of gelato, pizza, and cappuccino wafting through the air, and we often gave in to the temptations and tried them. I loved listening to the people when they spoke. The Italian language is like music to my ears; I could listen to it all day. I enjoyed the waterways, the canals, the shops, and the cobbled streets. It should have been romantic, but it was lost on us because we were *acting* as though we were on honeymoon.

We didn't have anything in common, including our language. I didn't speak Punjabi on a day-to-day basis, and his English wasn't good at all. I got irritated often because it seemed like he didn't know how to do anything. I had to do most things such as ordering the food and paying for it. I understand he came from a different country and had a difficult time adjusting, but Italy was foreign to me too. I had always dreamt of having a man who could take care of me and knew how to do just about everything. This certainly wasn't happening, and I just didn't have any compassion for him due to the circumstances that led me to being with him on this trip.

He was controlling and made sure to let me know he was the boss and didn't care about what I wanted. We had little arguments here and there about what we should do next, where to go, where to eat, and just about everything. One night in Rome, we went from one restaurant to another in search of food, but he didn't want pizza or pasta—he wanted burgers. We finally ordered food from McDonald's. I was annoyed that we had to eat at McDonald's on our honeymoon.

✳︎✳︎✳︎

In Rome, we visited the Vatican and St. Peter's Basilica. I felt as though I belonged there, and I've often wished I could live in Italy. The food is delicious, the people and their language are lovely, the country is beautiful, the art is magnificent, and the buildings are out of this world. It is a photographer's paradise.

Pope John Paul II was at the Vatican, and I got excited when someone told me we could be in the audience to see him. I jumped at the chance. My husband wasn't as keen about it as I was, but he went along with me. We lined up, and it wasn't long before we saw the Pope. I held out my hand when he passed me, and he kissed it. Pope John Paul II had blessed me.

My husband didn't stand with me, but he took photos with my camera, including when Pope John Paul II was close to me. I have of one or two pictures from the so-called "honeymoon." One image is of me in St. Mark's Square in Venice. Whenever I share it with anyone, I remind them that pictures aren't always what they seem. Someone can be in the most romantic place in the world and have a smile on their face, but it doesn't mean they are happy or feel lucky to be there.

There is a story behind every picture. I believe we all have to question reality to some degree. Don't always accept what you see. Probe and ask questions and you may be surprised what you find out. Reality isn't always as it appears in front of you.

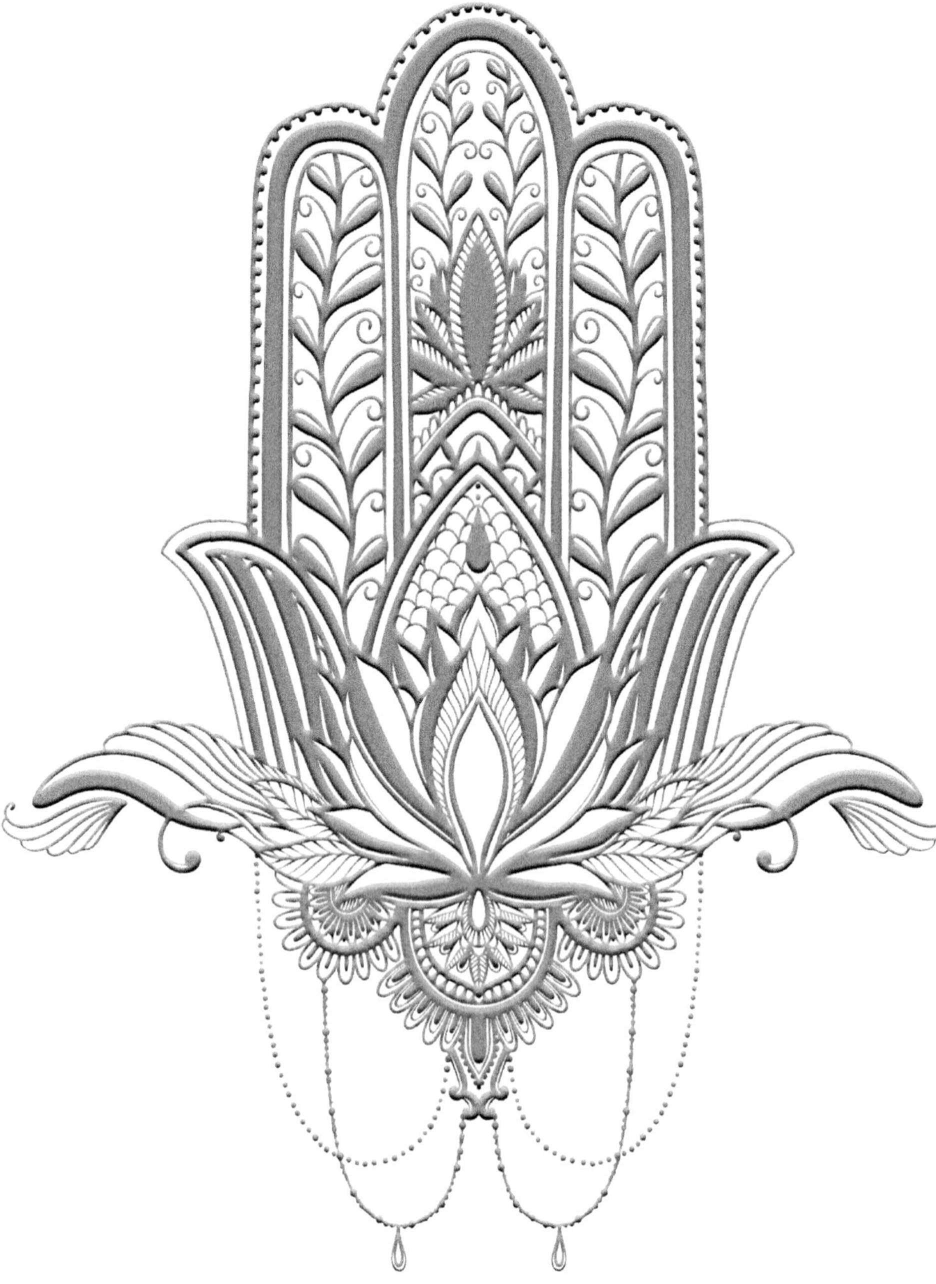

Return to Denmark and Our New Place

Once our honeymoon was over, we returned to our studio apartment. We had a big bed in the middle of the room and a sofa bed off to the side. The kitchen was across the hall, with a dining area to one side. It wasn't much, but at least we didn't have to share with Mr. Shergill's daughter and her husband anymore.

"Bik, I haven't changed my mind from what I told you on our honeymoon. I still don't want to be intimate with you again, and we need to sleep separately." I went to the sofa bed and pulled it out for myself.

He sighed in resignation. "Okay, Davinder. If that is what you want, I'll wait." He didn't seem happy about it, but I think he somewhat expected it, considering my aloofness while on our trip.

"Davinder, I asked you once before, but I'm going to ask again. Have you been with anyone else?"

"I haven't been with a man in the way you seem to expect me to answer. I *kissed* a man when I was in London. That's it. We didn't do anything else." I didn't want to reveal too much. I didn't feel he was entitled to it. He was an intruder in my life, a stranger I was forced to be with. Besides, he would have been furious if I had given him any further information about my relationship with Franz.

"London? When? Was it during our engagement?"

I sighed. "Yes, Bik, it was. I ran away because I didn't want to get married."

"You're lying. I would have known. Your mother would have told my family."

"What reason do I have to lie? It was my mother's idea not to tell anyone about it. You'll have to have this conversation with her. Go ahead. I'm sure she'll confirm my story now that I've told you the truth. I was too young when I agreed to the marriage, I was only fourteen. As I got older, I knew I couldn't go through with it, so I ran away to London. My family made me go back home. I was tricked and forced to continue with the marriage to you. I wished so much that I hadn't gone ahead with it. I'm really unhappy with this situation."

"So if you haven't been with another man, why was there no blood on the sheets on our wedding night? I'm having a hard time trusting you."

"I have no idea why there wasn't blood on the sheets. I'm telling you I haven't been with anyone else. I was a virgin the day we married. I don't care if you don't believe me!" I yelled indignantly.

We sat in silence for a few moments and stared at one another. He studied me intently, almost as if he was trying to determine if I was being honest with him.

I shifted my weight on the couch and tried to get comfortable so we could continue the conversation.

"What about you, Bik? Have you been with another woman?"

His eyes widened as if I'd offended him. "Absolutely not, Davinder, but I experimented with other men."

I sucked in a quick breath. "You *what*? Really?!"

I couldn't have cared less that he'd been with other men or women, as I really didn't care about *him* at all. I was livid that he thought it was okay for him to do as he pleased but refused to take my word about the sheets. He didn't believe I was a virgin, but I knew it was the absolute truth. Based on his line of questioning and what he'd revealed, he seemingly thought it was only wrong to play around with someone of the *opposite* sex before marriage. To me, regardless if it was someone of the same sex or the opposite sex, it was still fooling around.

This argument was a big deal. He'd questioned my integrity when I had done almost everything according to custom. I didn't like it, but I'd followed the rules and waited until my wedding night. I was appalled that I had ascribed to this cultural expectation. Look where it had gotten me!

Even when I'd had the chance to be with Franz in London, we didn't take it the whole way. I kept thinking of how I was supposed to behave, and I tried my best to do what I thought was right. In that moment, I regretted my decision. My culture dictated how I was supposed to behave, and it had become so ingrained in me that even when I could have escaped it, I was imprisoned by it.

The fact I'd been forced to marry a man who didn't believe me was beyond my comprehension, and I was livid about it. I was also angered by his double standards, with him thinking it was okay to do what he liked and trying to come across as pure and innocent. To me, he had been with someone sexually, and it was the same whether he had been with a man or a woman. I certainly wasn't jealous he'd been with someone, but I was very annoyed that he didn't believe I hadn't. It was almost as though the sheets "proved" I was guilty, no matter what I said, but his own admission of being with someone was okay because he had been with someone of the same sex.

We weren't on the same page, and it only added to my frustration and disappointment of being forced to be with him. We thought differently; we didn't click. He not only had double standards, but our Indian culture allowed him to be held to different standards than women. Men could sleep around before marriage and weren't considered "soiled" or "unmarriageable." However, if a woman were to fool around and it was found out, she wasn't marriage material. I had to call home and let my mum know I wasn't happy. The phone rang three times before she answered.

"Hello?"

"Mum, it's Davinder."

"Hi, Davinder. How are you?"

"Mum," I blurted out, "I'm not happy with him. We are too different and have nothing in common with each other. I don't like him, and I don't want to be with him."

"Davinder, it will take a little while for you to get used to each other, and it's just a question of time. You have to give it more time!"

"No, I don't want to!" I insisted. "I never wanted this. I don't get along with him. I just can't take his attitude. He's too controlling."

"Stop, Davinder. You're not giving him a chance. Let me speak to him."

"He's not here right now. I called you while he is out, or else he'd probably be really annoyed."

She refused to listen to my pleas for help. I desperately wished to be released from this marriage I had never wanted. It was clear I wouldn't get anywhere with my calls to my mother.

My mum would never say, "Davinder, of course you should leave him if you don't feel anything for him. Just come home. He will have to learn to deal with it." After all, why would she?

What mattered most to her was that I had to make it work no matter what. There was no option to get out of it. It wasn't a possibility. Whatever her reasons for staying in her own unhappy marriage, she'd obviously ascribed to trying to make a marriage work and certainly hadn't arranged mine so it could fail so quickly. I soon learned my husband called Mum behind my back and reported I wasn't giving him a chance.

We had to find work so we could pay the rent on the apartment. I got hired at Burger King in central Copenhagen prior to the honeymoon and started working there upon our return. I worked there for several months. I was happy to have a job and be independent. I loved my time at Burger King and enjoyed the camaraderie. I often hung out with the other employees on our days off.

Mr. Shergill's daughter and husband owned a small shop and offered my husband a job. His English wasn't good enough for him to get a job anywhere else, and his Danish was non-existent. In order to gain employment in Denmark, applicants had to speak either English or Danish—sometimes, both languages were required. I had been disqualified from several jobs because I didn't speak Danish. Luckily, Burger King didn't have that in their hiring policies.

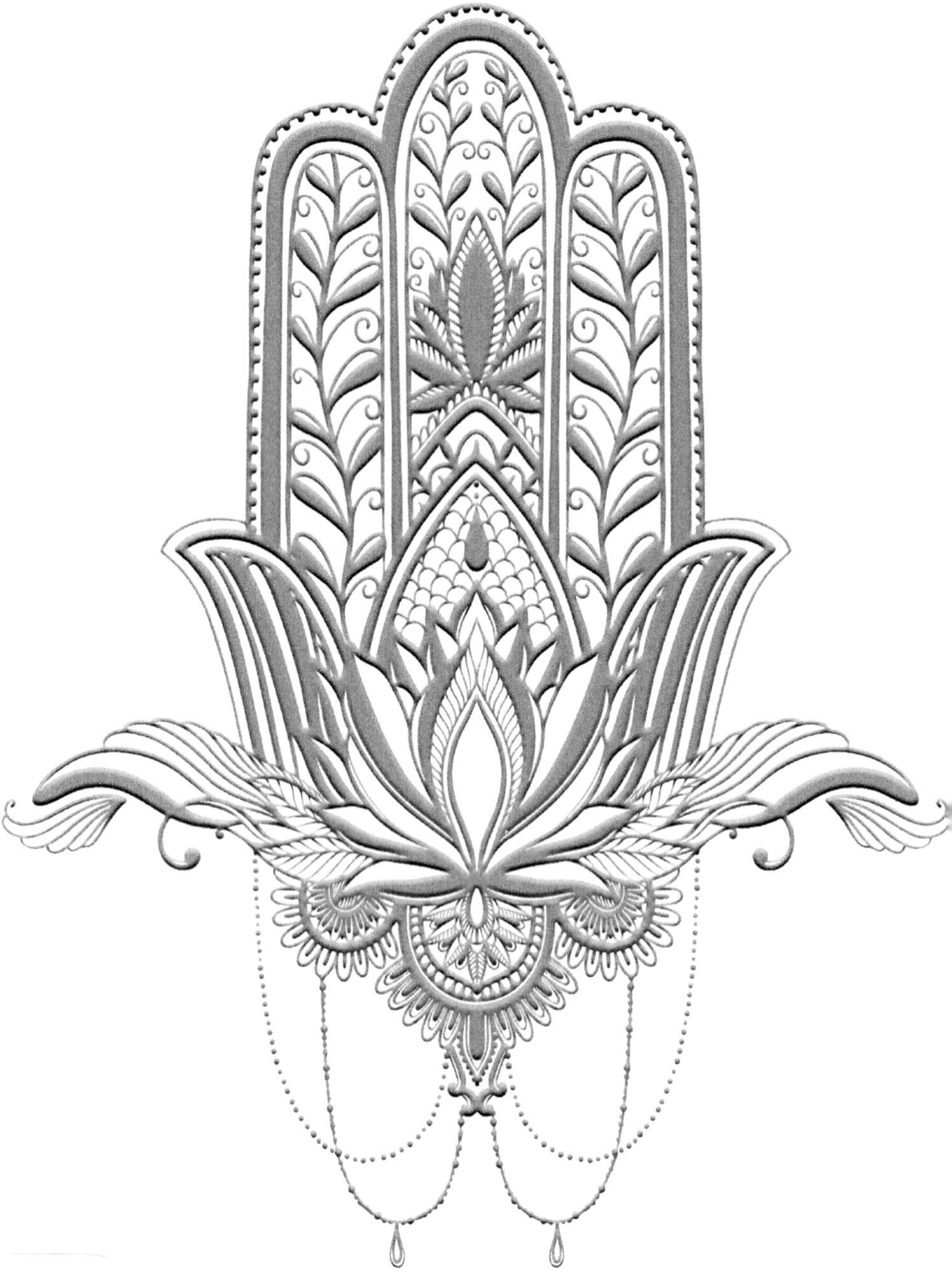

The Control Freak

It had been over a week and a half since I had gotten married. I took the bus to work most times, but I could walk if I had to. I applied eyeliner and lipstick, the only makeup I wanted to put on now that I was married and allowed to wear it. I couldn't believe it when my husband told me it wasn't necessary for me to wear makeup to work because I wasn't with him. Apparently, my wearing makeup was for his benefit and not for the benefit of anyone else. No one at work had to see me with makeup because I might look too pretty, and what was the point of being dolled up for them?

He also told me I had to be careful about who I talked to on the bus. For example, I was to ask a woman for directions, not a man. His need for control infuriated me. I knew instinctively I could not be with a man like him; I don't know how I knew it because I didn't have common knowledge of men. I didn't know much about good or evil men, but in my opinion, he fell into the evil category.

The following week, two weeks into our marriage, I announced I wanted a divorce. I was absolutely certain the relationship wasn't going to work—I didn't want it. I didn't want him, had never wanted him, and I was determined to exercise my choices and desires.

"Bik", I'm disgusted you didn't believe me when I told you I was a virgin when I married you. I find that appalling. In fact, there's something I need to let you know. I want a divorce."

"What? A divorce! Are you out of your mind, Davinder? It's only been two weeks. You have to give this time. I will give you whatever time you need".

"No, Bik, I don't want to stay in this marriage. I really have to get out of it. I knew I didn't want to be in it *before* we got married. I've already told you that. I also knew I would want to get divorced as soon as possible. Really, I shouldn't have given in—it was a huge mistake."

"You can't do this, Davinder. Your mum and dad will not be happy with you, or with me. We have to make this work. Give me more time, Davinder. You can't give up so easily."

"I can, and I will. I don't want any of this; I never have. I'm not going to change my mind, Bik. I want to get out of this as soon as possible. You should marry someone who can love you. I can never love you. I'm not attracted to you and didn't want to be married to you to begin with."

"You will *not* divorce me. If you get away from me, I will kill myself and come back and haunt you."

I was starting to feel scared and yelled back at him, "Don't threaten me. That isn't nice of you. You're trying to scare me, and that's a very sick thing to say."

He stormed out of the studio and didn't return for several hours.

One day, I was clearing the tables at Burger King when I noticed a stranger watching me intently. He smiled and approached me near one of the trashcans as I emptied some trays.

"If you don't mind me asking, what's your name?"

"It's Davinder, but why do you want to know?" I wanted more of an answer from him than I should have. Perhaps I was ready to flirt. I didn't care that I was married because I didn't consider it a real marriage.

"You're really pretty, but I'm sure you know that. I bet you hear that from guys all the time. If it's okay with you, I'd like to get to know you more." His smile broadened and reached his kind eyes.

"What's *your* name?" I ventured, matching his boldness.

"I'm Peter. May I take you out sometime soon?"

I took a deep breath and chose honesty in that moment. "I'm married, Peter, although unhappily. In fact, it's been just over two weeks. It was an arranged marriage; I didn't want it. I've already told my husband I want a divorce."

"Would you like to tell me more about it over coffee sometime?"

I nodded and smiled. "I would like that."

Peter was older than me—I was eighteen, and he was thirty-one. He looked very Scandinavian with his curly blond hair. He was polite and smiled a lot, a stark contrast to my husband, and he seemed happier and much more relaxed.

After my shift the next day, I told him about my situation at a nearby café.

"I'm miserable, Peter." I shook my head and stared at my trembling hands. "I hate my arrangement with my husband. Our families pushed us into the marriage because of antiquated traditions in my culture, but it's so wrong. I want out."

"I would like to help you, Davinder. This isn't fair for you. It's awful that your family did this to you, and now you're in a strange country being forced to suffer through it alone. You aren't alone anymore. I'm here for you, day or night. You can call on me anytime. Do you promise that you won't hesitate to reach out to me?"

The fact he'd asked me like this endeared him more to me than anyone could imagine. To have someone on my side was what I needed more than anything else.

Over the next few weeks, Peter often came into Burger King for meals or just to sit with a cup of tea and an apple pie. We went for coffee one other time, and he gave me his address and told me he didn't live far from me. I put the slip of paper with his information in a section of my bag where it wouldn't fall out. Deep down, I knew I might need to call on him.

Meanwhile, back at home, the situation between Bik and I got worse. We were barely speaking to one another and carried on living like this for another month. Finally, I found out he had called my mum again and complained about me and the distance I had put between us. Mum was going to send my dad to Denmark so he could talk some sense into me or help us out with our situation. I found this out from Bik. He told me about my dad's impending arrival.

My Dad's Arrival and the Unforgivable Incident

(Warning: This chapter may be uncomfortable for some people because it describes a very traumatic experience. If you have experienced a situation such as rape, violence, or sexual abuse, you may want to skip this chapter.)

My father arrived in Copenhagen nearly six weeks into my marriage.

"Dad, I'm not happy with him," I blurted out within minutes of his arrival and after my husband had gone out to get something. "I can't stay with him."

"You just need more time together and perhaps guidance from elders. It might be best for you both to be in England with the family. You're all on your own here, and neither of you know what to do. Family can help."

"No, Dad, that's *not* going to help! I don't want to be with him. We have nothing in common," I insisted.

"You need to give it more time, Davinder," he repeated.

It was clear he didn't want to hear my pleas for my release from the marriage that had become my prison. It was as if he thought I'd blindly obey anything he said. He was just like Mum. They didn't want to hear my objections. I was supposed to be agreeable and give in to what they wanted for me.

"Listen, I'm going to go for a drink. I'll take Bik with me."

My dad left shortly afterward, and I stayed home.

A few hours later, my husband entered the apartment.

"Where's Dad?"

"Still drinking at the bar."

As he got closer to me, the stench of alcohol rolled of him in waves. An angry glint in his eye made it clear things weren't going to go well.

Finally, he spoke in Punjabi, "You're going to get what you deserve. You're a bad girl. Even your dad is upset with our situation, but you don't care. You don't care about anything or anyone but yourself! I am mad about everything! Your treatment of me is appalling, and if I can't have you, no one else can either!" he bellowed.

During our short time together, I'd never seen him behave that way. The alcohol on his breath grew more putrid the closer he came.

He turned on some music and set the volume high. Something was wrong. Dread welled up inside me, and I was certain something awful was about to happen. He advanced toward where I sat on my bed and pushed me backward on the mattress. Panic rushed through my veins as my stomach churned. He got on top of me and held me down with his heavy weight. I struggled against him but soon became weak. He slapped me a couple of times and placed his hands on my neck and began to strangle me.

"I've had enough of you. If you ever get away from me, I'm going to come back as a ghost and haunt you for the rest of my life!" He had said this to me before, and hearing it again was just as terrifying as it was the first time.

A tremendous chill rushed through me. Talking about ghosts implied something was going to happen to me. In that moment, I was so terrified that I didn't realize he was talking about *himself* coming back as a ghost. My face stung from his slaps, and I could barely breathe. I hadn't realized he was so powerful, but his rage gave him the strength he needed to completely overpower me.

"I have every right to sleep with you, and you are going to let me do whatever I want to right now!"

He squeezed his hands harder on my neck, and I knew instinctively this was it. If I didn't give in to his demands, I would die.

"I'm sorry," I sobbed. "I will do whatever you want. I'm really sorry for hurting you. Please believe me. I know now that I made a mistake—a huge mistake. I promise I won't leave you. I'll be a much better wife."

He relaxed and released me. "Take off your clothes."

I quickly did as I was told while he removed his pants. He got on top of me, and I had to give in to him, succumbing to his need for sexual intercourse.

"I'm sorry," I cried. I begged for forgiveness because he was rough and still angry with me. "I'm so sorry. I will be a much better wife. I'm really sorry for not being nice to you and putting you through everything you've gone through. I've been really bad."

I was uncertain if he'd do something else to me. I had to endure this monster and his evil actions on my body, the body that wanted nothing to do with him. I had no choice but to let him have full control; doing anything to stop him could have led to my death.

He calmed down and put his clothes back on after he got what he wanted. I dressed myself as quickly as I could while my head reeled with what I had just experienced. I had to continue playing smart with him until I was sure I was safe.

"You're going to have to be a much better wife than you've been. All this nonsense of you leaving me will stop, do you understand?"

I nodded.

He towered over me as I sat on the bed. "You will start listening to me and make more of an effort. Do you understand?"

"I will. I will do whatever you want and be a good wife," I promised again. I needed him to believe me so I could ensure my safety.

He finally turned down the music. "I will go get your dad, and you should get ready for his return. Don't tell him what just happened, okay?"

"I won't. I promise."

As soon as he stepped out the door, I had my first chance to attempt to process everything. I felt so violated. I was cold and in pain, but not from my neck or what he had just done to me. I felt an inner pain I couldn't comprehend. How had I gotten myself into such a terrible situation? I wrapped my hands in a crisscross fashion over my shoulders, giving myself some warmth and comfort.

His words ran through my mind. *"I will come back as a ghost and haunt you."*

None of it was right. That monster had raped me, nearly killed me, and terrorized me! I hurt deep inside and began sobbing hysterically. All the odds were stacked against me: I lived on the top floor of a building with hardly any neighbors, he'd turned up the music, I had been alone with a madman, and I had been forced to marry him without knowing what he was capable of. It was too much for me to handle.

I couldn't dwell in self-pity; I had to act quickly. I'd managed to save my life, but I hadn't made it through the entire situation unscathed. I could barely digest everything.

How did I let this happen?

Why had this happened to me?

Was there anything I could have done differently to stop him?

I put my head in my hands and let out several sobs, not giving a damn if I was too loud. Even if they hadn't heard my cries during the attack, why hadn't someone called the police to report the loud music? I wiped away my tears but more took their place as they flowed down my cheeks. I tried to get a grip on myself; I had to think quickly. I was going to tell my dad. He would make everything right; he had to. After all, I was his little girl, and he was here to help. He was the only one who could protect me.

About an hour later, my dad came back and said my husband was on his way but had to stop at the store first.

"Dad, Bik just raped me! You have to help! I don't want anything to do with him; he's a monster! He just strangled me and tried to kill me!"

My dad looked at me blankly and didn't bat an eyelid. It was almost as if my words hadn't registered properly, but I wasn't prepared for what followed.

"He's your husband. He has every right to do that to you!"

My dad didn't want to help his daughter when she pleaded for him to step in and protect her and punish the man they had forced her to marry. Perhaps they hadn't realized what he was like before, but now that I'd told my dad, couldn't he see this behavior was completely unacceptable?

I would have loved it if he had hugged me and said, "Don't worry, Davinder, I'm your dad. I will take care of him. How dare he do this to you!" But no, my dad didn't care; my husband was the priority. He was their son now, and since sons were more important than daughters, they were going to take his side over mine.

I had no one else. My parents had placed me in a strange country with a husband of *their* choice. He sexually assaulted me, and my dad said it's his *right*! *They* made him my husband, not me. My parents had given him the *right* to do whatever he wanted to me. I was only eighteen, but I knew I shouldn't be controlled, abused, frightened, or subject to being terrorized by a bully.

"Dad, what are you saying?" I cried. "You can't mean that! You know that's not right, that's not fair! Bik had no right to do that to me, even if we're married. I never wanted him to be my husband, and you know that!"

He didn't respond. Within a few minutes, my husband returned.

I began to plot how I would get away that night. It was time for me to escape from my evil husband and the dad who had let me down and couldn't protect his own daughter. My husband acted like nothing had happened, and my dad never approached him to ask if he had just violated me, hurt me, and almost killed me. No. Nothing of the sort happened. They didn't talk about it at all.

I was deeply hurt and felt like no one cared. I was just an object; I didn't matter. My pain or feelings didn't matter. But this stupid marriage mattered, and this stupid marriage had bothered me from the day I got engaged. I wanted out from underneath all of it, especially now.

An idea popped into my head.

"Dad, would you like some tea?"

"Yes, Bindi. Tea would be nice."

"Would you like some too, Bik?"

"Yes, please."

I went across the hall to the kitchen and put some water in a pan to boil. This was my chance; I just needed my bag. I managed to go back into the room and grab my bag without either of them seeing me.

For once, it was nice not to be noticed.

The Second Escape

With my bag in hand, I moved slowly and silently. My heart was beating so fast, I worried they'd hear it and catch me before I reached the door at the end of the hallway. I opened and closed it behind me as quietly as I could. I was anxious they might come out of the studio and see me from the other end of the hallway. If I got a glimpse of them just before the door closed, I was doomed, but I didn't see them. I kept moving.

A hundred steps would lead me to freedom. For the second time in my life, I was running away. I was afraid I was being followed or that they knew I was gone, so I ran. I could have tripped at any moment, but I attempted to calm my nerves and finally reached the bottom. Flinging open the door and stepping outside, I hailed a taxi and asked the driver to take me to Peter's house.

Panic weighed heavily in my chest. What if Peter wasn't home? What if he didn't want me there?

For the second time in my life, I felt the same fear as I wondered if my dad and husband knew I was gone.

The taxi came to a stop in front of an apartment building. I quickly paid my fare, grabbed my bag, and headed for the front door. I rang the bell and waited. Peter's voice came through the intercom, and shortly after I identified myself, he opened the door and hugged me tightly.

"Davinder, what are you doing here? It is wonderful to see you!"

Relief washed over me at the sight of the joy on his face. I clutched at him tightly, needing his support now more than ever. "Peter, I need your help. Can I please stay with you for a few days? I left my husband and have nowhere else to go."

He sighed and offered a sad smile. "Of course. Let's go upstairs."

His one-bedroom flat was huge compared to my studio. He even had his own toilet and a shower. I looked forward to using a toilet I didn't have to share with neighbors.

Peter made coffee and told me I could stay as long as I liked—his home was my home too. I was so thankful for his kindness and generosity. Although we'd talked when I was at work and had gone for coffee a few times, we were still practically strangers.

"Peter, I was raped by my husband. He almost killed me." I collapsed into his arms and sobbed. When I gathered myself, I continued. "He was strangling me, Peter, and I had to give in to save myself because I knew he was going to hurt and possibly kill me. I had to tell him I was sorry for everything. I hate him. I am so angry! Peter, how could this have happened? I need help!" I was a mess. Tears flowed freely down my face, no matter how many times I wiped them away.

Peter was furious. "Davinder, you have to report the rape to the police. We are not going to let him get away with this."

I knew he was right. I could barely believe what was happening. It was like a bad dream, a nightmare, but I wouldn't wake up from this one to realize it was just a dream. This was reality, *my* horrible reality.

My dad should have insisted I go to the police and file a report, but to families like mine, it wasn't rape—rape or sex with your wife was a man's right. Pushing aside thoughts of my dad and my disappointment, I picked up the phone and dialed the police. They told me I had to come in to fill out a report and be tested. Peter drove me to the station. I filed the report, but I didn't agree to do the test. It was too invasive, and I was scared. I told the police I hadn't been intimate with my husband for almost the entire duration of the marriage, but my husband had forced himself on me and raped me. The officers asked about him, where he worked, and where he could be found. I gave them all the information I had.

I'm not sure if the police ever found him or questioned him. I never went back to him though. I later found out my dad had left for England the next day.

Return to the Apartment

I took a few days off from work and told the manager my situation over the phone. They were very understanding. Once I returned to work, I feared my husband would show up, but he never did. I had a strange feeling, like I was being followed. I think he had mentioned during the attack that he'd had someone following me—one of the Pakistani taxi drivers.

I needed my things from my apartment: my gold jewelry, my clothes, and my school certificates, including my O-Level and GCSE Certificates. While I was still going to school in England, I had ordered a Memory and Concentration course from Dr. Bruno Furst. I had brought it with me to Denmark, as this was one of my prized possessions. I also had a response to a letter I wrote to Buckingham Palace asking if I could attend the wedding of Princess Diana and Prince Charles in 1981. They thanked me for my inquiry on Palace letterhead, but they deeply regretted they could not take any more guests.

My managers offered to escort me to my apartment and stand guard while I got the things I needed. We all went together one morning and were shocked to see the walls had been damaged. It seemed my husband had taken a sharp object and scraped the walls, leaving ugly scratches in the paint.

To my dismay, I found that most of my belongings were gone, including my school certificates, the Dr. Bruno Furst collection, the letter from Buckingham Palace, most of my new Indian clothes I had not yet worn, gold jewelry, leather pants, and pictures. Even my pictures with the Pope were gone. I was so upset. Those were *my* things, not his!

He had damaged the wall to spite me because he knew my money, or my mother's money, was put down for the deposit. I didn't get my deposit back because the landlord was rightfully mad and withheld it. My managers stayed with me while I retrieved what little I could. We left the apartment about an hour later.

I called home to let Mum know he had taken my things.

"He's your husband. He has the right."

My parents didn't care about my feelings or my possessions, and they didn't respect the fact their daughter was wronged. In their eyes, I was the perpetrator.

I had caused this. *I* had wronged him, and now *I* was to suffer the consequences of my actions. He was their beloved son, and he needed their help and understanding. It was ridiculous. Mum could have gotten my belongings if she had asked him, but she didn't bother. I didn't know what he had done with my things. I thought he might have given the gold and my clothes to his sister-in-law or someone else in his family. He had no right, but I didn't know what to do.

I followed up with the police in Copenhagen and told them I wanted my husband deported. He had no right to be here, and he had come here just to marry me and use me to gain citizenship. They told me they would look for him and try to get my possessions back. I don't believe they were able to find him. I never saw him again, but I got in touch with a divorce lawyer and started proceedings in Denmark. It took over three years to finalize the divorce, and then it was transferred to lawyers in England where it was finally declared on paper that I was divorced as of September 21st, 1990.

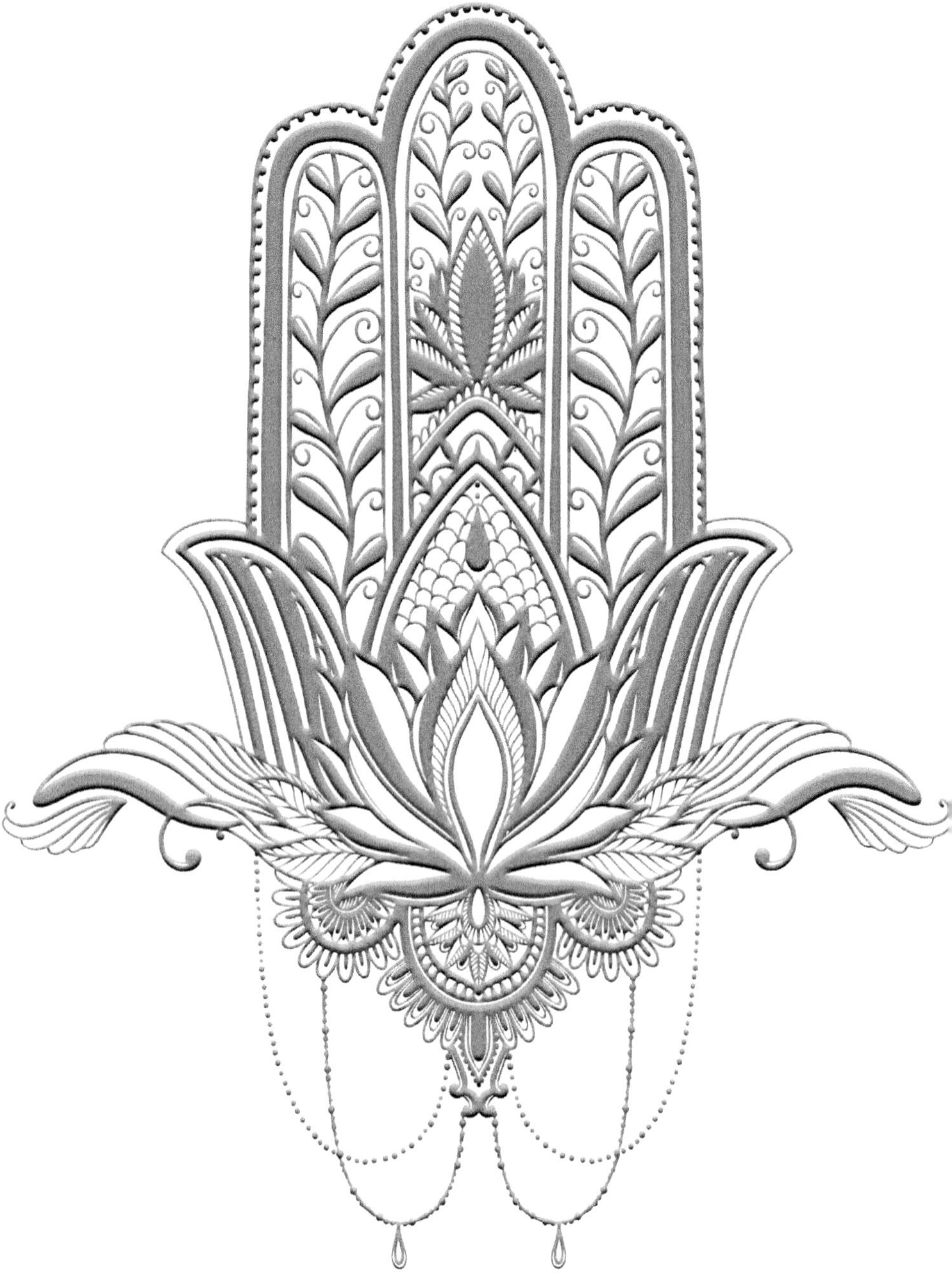

Freedom at Last

At last, I had my freedom. In a way, it was how I had planned it. I knew I would get away from him after the marriage. My parents wouldn't listen to me when I said I didn't want it. I was pushed into it because of family shame and the fact that so many people were waiting for it to happen. It was a matter of family honor.

In the Punjabi culture, family honor is so important to everyone that no one wants to let down the family or bring shame to them. In most cases, the child is an object that has no real feelings or needs. The parents' needs are most important and must be considered above all else. I realized this and knew the only way to escape again was to be away from my family and in another country.

My first attempt to get away wasn't successful because I gave in to my mum's guilt trip and returned home. Escaping to London had been the right thing for me to do. I should have stayed and never looked back, but I weakened. I went home and delivered what my family expected of me.

The pressure mounted, and I felt I couldn't escape again unless I did it on my terms. I now realize that agreeing to the marriage was a terrible idea and not the best path to freedom. I succumbed to the pressure and did what everyone else wanted me to do.

Even though I ultimately escaped the marriage, what price did I pay? I gave up my innocence and was raped, strangled, and nearly killed by my husband. He terrorized and tormented me and then stole all my belongings—things that had personal meaning to me.

My own dad didn't rescue me when he could have. Both parents had let me down and weren't there for me when I pleaded for their help several times. The scars of my abuse stayed with me, locked inside, and only came out when I gave in to the deep thinking of the situation. For a long time, I blocked it out just to escape it. It wasn't at all okay for an eighteen-year-old to have to cope alone and be in danger due to being married to a stranger.

Peter and I were together for almost a year. He was refreshing for me. He was kind, supportive, and not at all controlling—the complete opposite of my husband. He was open and trusting, very calm, and he was my best friend. I had fun with him and thought I was in love for the first time in my life. I look back now and realize even though I cared deeply for Peter and loved him, I was not *in* love with him. I think what I felt was appreciation and gratitude. He was a truly wonderful person though. We were together for almost a year.

I finally called home to talk to my mum one day. When she heard my voice, she became icy toward me.

"Why are you calling me? There is nothing for us to talk about if you're not going to listen to what I say."

"Mum, I don't want to go back to him; I can't. You know what he did to me. He had no right to do that. He tried to kill me."

"You drove him to that. He's your husband, and you should have given him more of a chance. I'm going to send your auntie to visit you. Perhaps *she* can talk some sense into you. Maybe you can go back to Germany with her and clear things up in your head and change your mind."

"Mum, I'm not going back. I don't want to go to Germany; I'm fine where I am. I don't need anyone to come talk to me or convince me to go back to Bik. I'm *never* going back to him." I'd already explained this to her multiple times, but she never listened to me. "I'm happy here with Peter."

She hung up on me as soon as the words left my lips.

It upset me when our conversations didn't go well. It hurt more when she hung up on me. It took a lot for me to recover from each conversation that ended poorly.

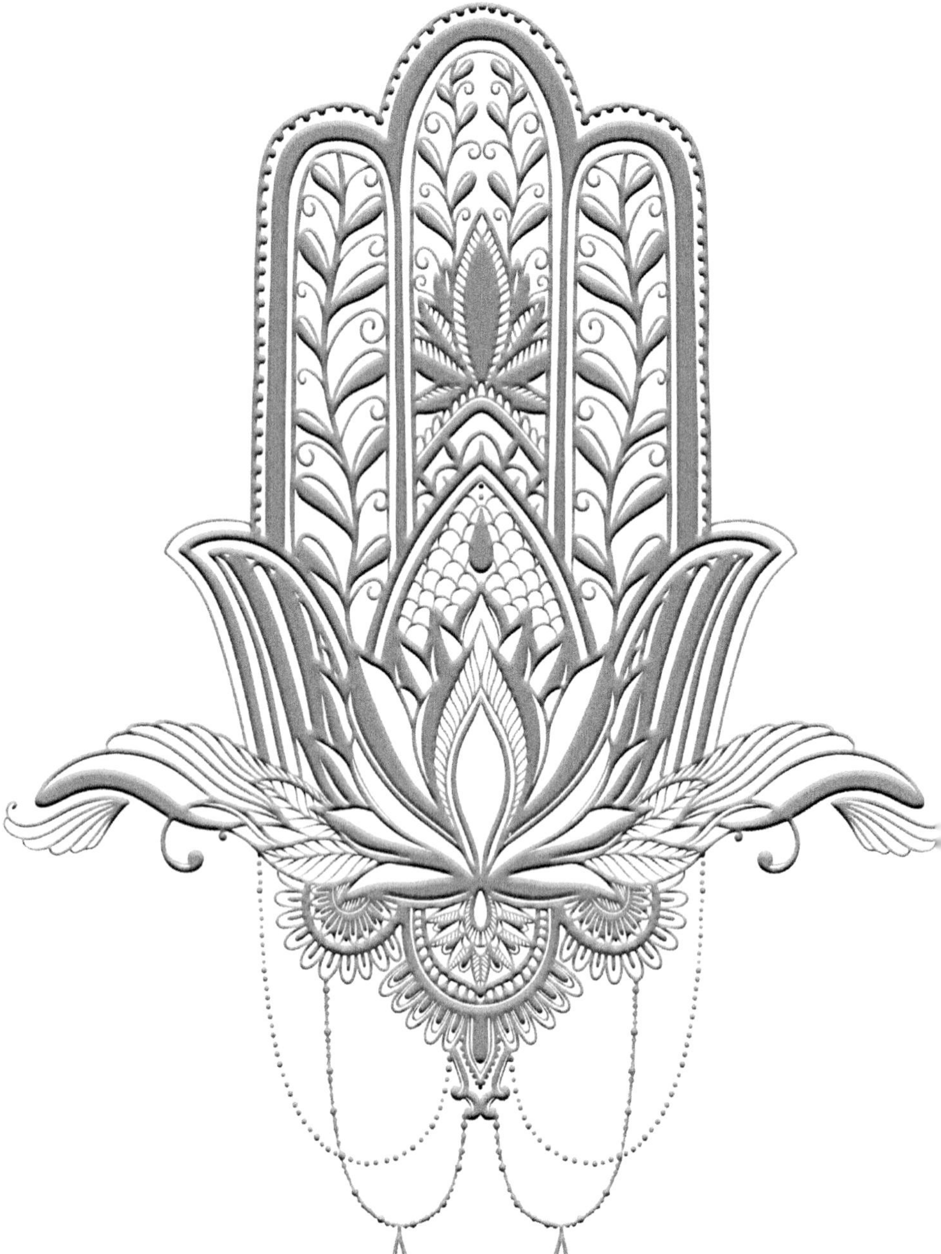

Two More Forced Marriages in the Family

While I was in Denmark and after I left my husband, Mum had Mandeep married to the girl from India. I wasn't invited and wasn't talking to my mother at the time, so I didn't attend the wedding. Unfortunately, it didn't work out well. He and his wife had no chemistry, and he certainly wasn't happy with her. He told my mum about his unhappiness many times before she finally listened to him. Surprisingly, she agreed with my brother.

It was good that she saw his marriage had to end, but it was unfortunate because his ex-wife was sent back to India. Once a woman gets divorced and must return to India, her life is ruined. In India, and many other places, it's fine if a man remarries. When it comes to the woman, however, there's a stigma attached to her because she's been with another man. She's now considered "untouchable" and undesirable material for remarriage.

Mum spent so much money on my marriage, including the cost for the clothes and gold, plus the honeymoon. On top of that, she had the expenses for my brother, the gold for his bride and her clothes, as well as new clothes for my brother. They went on a honeymoon but didn't have a good time either. I wasn't surprised.

My mum had wasted so much money on our marriages, and she was about to organize a third for my sister who is a year and a half younger than me. It's not just about the money though. Our lives were damaged, and the pain inflicted on all of us was completely unnecessary.

All three weddings happened within six months to a year of each other. My sister's wedding was in Germany, and again, I did not get to attend. My sister married the nephew of my uncle who was married to my auntie (Mum's sister). My sister was related to my auntie by blood, and her husband was related to my uncle by blood, but the two of them weren't blood relatives.

Not surprisingly, my sister's marriage also ended badly. She didn't like her husband and didn't want to work at the marriage. I don't blame her. I would understand the expectation to save our marriages or make them work if we had made our own choices, but when we had little or no choice, why should we work for something none of us wanted? My sister's failed marriage was even more of a shame and embarrassment than mine and my brother's because this was my uncle's nephew and my auntie's niece. They each had a family member whose life had turned upside down.

I'd like to say I can imagine the torment my mother must have gone through and how ashamed she must have been of all of us. She'd wasted a lot of money on three failed marriages that had crumbled within six months or so of each other. I can't imagine how she kept herself going or how she held up her head in her community and within the family. It must have been hard for her. I feel for her agony during this horrible time, even though everything she did was of her own doing. However, she reaped what she sowed.

I'm not asking for forgiveness for what I did and for what she experienced with my brother and sister. Still, no one deserves to see all their dreams shattered and money gone down the drain. She must have compared herself to her brothers, who were able to get their children arranged marriages. She must have wondered where she went wrong.

According to my mum, I was the problem. I was the one who started everything from the time I ran away and wanted to avoid the marriage, to the time I left my husband and didn't give him a chance. She told me on the phone that my brother and sister had copied me, and that I was a bad example. This was my fault. I was astounded. This was yet another example of how Mum practiced gaslighting on us all through her control and psychological abuse.

I later learned my mum endured even more heartache while I was in Denmark. Kuljeet had run away before she was eighteen and before her marriage in Germany. It was obvious Kuljeet was reacting to the excessive control and didn't want to get married. My family had to deal with her not wanting anything to do with them once they located her. Her situation was different from mine because she was a minor at the time, but eventually she went back home.

My youngest sister, Sabina, had a very different experience than our other siblings and me. We all had forced marriages. Sabina had an arranged marriage. Arranged marriages work if organized properly and with full consent of both parties. Since Sabina is the youngest, and my mum had already witnessed the failures of our marriages, she arranged Sabina's differently. I thank God for that! Sabina was allowed to go to a restaurant and movie theaters with her fiancé. Her fiancé was Indian but from England, and he wasn't born and raised in India, which also helped. They had a lot more in common. Since they had gone on at least two dates and had a chance to get to know each other, they also realized they were attracted to one another and wanted the marriage. This led to the success of their marriage. This is the way it should be. This is the way it should have been arranged for all of us.

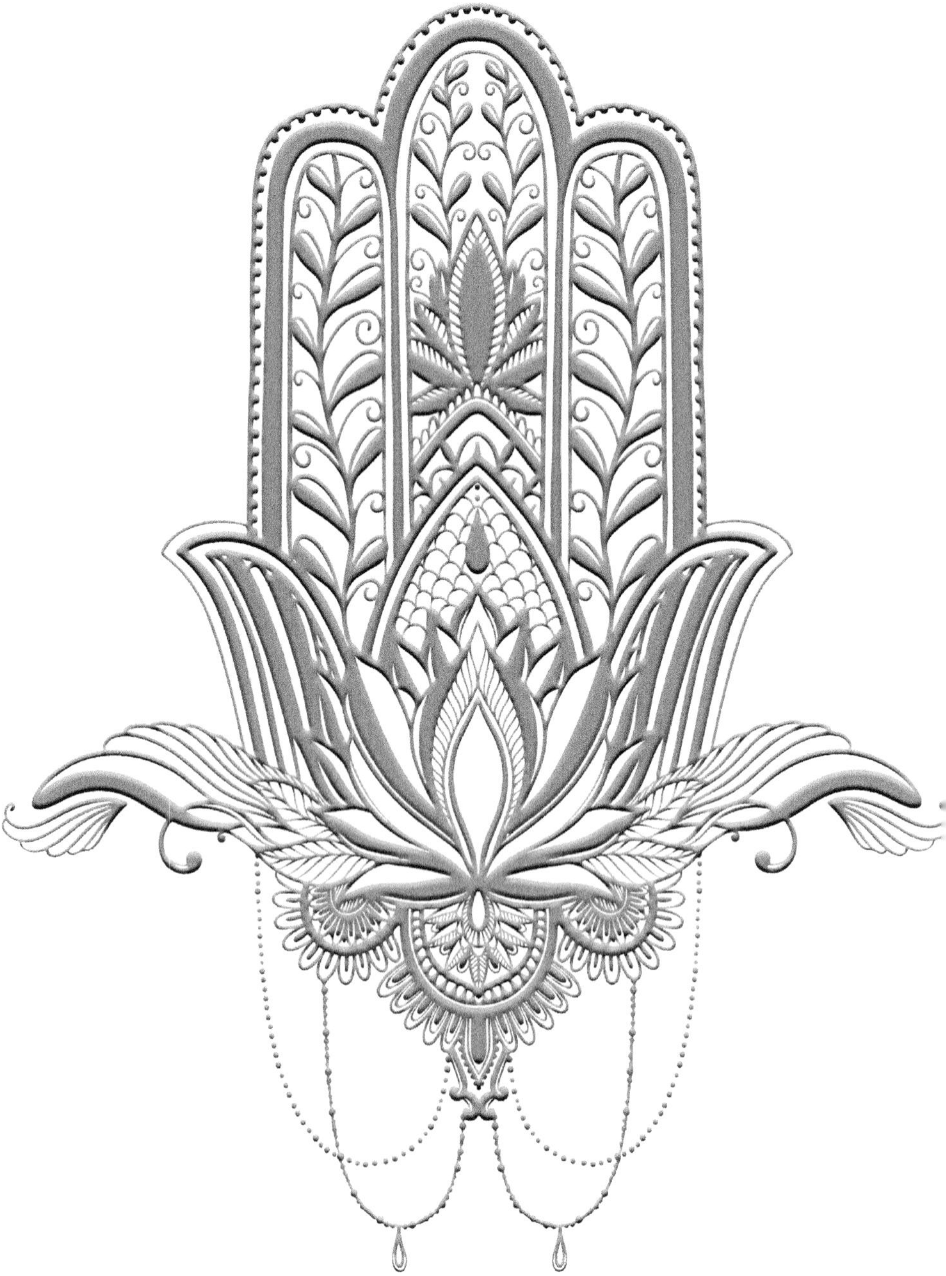

The Trip to Germany

After the phone call with my mother and within a few weeks of my leaving my husband, my auntie and uncle from Germany showed up in Burger King. They talked me into going back with them, and I told Peter I would try to return in a few weeks.

My sister was in Germany at that time. I'm not sure if this was before or after her wedding. I don't remember her husband being there, so I think it was before she got married. Perhaps she was sent there early, just as I was when I was sent to Denmark. My sister and I didn't talk too much about my failed marriage; we weren't into talking about personal things at all at that point in our lives. I believe this stemmed from our upbringing. It took me a long time to open up to anyone about my personal life.

My uncle tried to find me a job and get me settled in Germany with them. I liked my auntie and uncle very much and loved seeing my four-year-old cousin and his little brother, but my heart wasn't set for being in Germany. I missed Peter and wanted to return to him. I told my auntie and uncle I had to go back to Denmark. They weren't happy to see me go, but I think they understood.

Mum was furious when she found out I had gone back to Peter. I called her after arriving in Denmark, but she hung up on me. The same thing happened when I called a few weeks later. I realized my mum didn't want to have anything to do with me. It was really upsetting.

Before too long, I heard from either my uncle or my auntie that I had the option to marry my sister's husband because their marriage hadn't worked out. I was shocked! I couldn't believe what they were saying or suggesting! How could I marry my sister's husband? She had been with him already, and why would I want to be associated with him at all?

Within my culture, it is common to marry a sibling's spouse if so required. If a sibling passes away, another sister can replace her by marrying her sister's husband. She can help raise the children, and it ensures he's no longer without a wife. However, since I was raised in England, it just didn't feel right to me. Of course, I declined.

The Trip to Australia

Toward the end of 1987, I bought a one-way ticket to Australia after talking to Peter about it. He was really good about giving me the freedom to make my own choices and allowing me space to explore. He knew I was a lot younger than him and didn't want to tie me down. I had always been fascinated with Australia and watched anything to do with it on TV, including *Neighbors*.

I left Denmark with very little money—probably the equivalent of $250—so I stayed in a youth hostel in Sydney for a few weeks because it was cheap. When I began to run low on funds, I picked up odd jobs here and there, including one where I sold oil paintings door to door. I made enough money to travel and was on my way again. Initially, I purchased coach tickets to different cities such as Brisbane, where I spent the most time out of my one-year stay in Australia.

I got adventurous later and hitchhiked across the country. I was able to visit the majority of Australia without spending so much money on bus tickets. Hitchhiking can be dangerous, though, and I had a few close calls with my safety, especially when truck drivers pulled over in the evening to rest. They slept in the back of their trucks and expected me to join them. I wasn't comfortable with that, and one of them took deep offense to my refusal and threw me off his truck in the middle of the night. I had to hold out my hand and get a ride with someone else.

I met one of my dearest friends, Mindy, while I was in Australia. She was also Indian and from England. Sadly, we've lost touch over the years, but we had a lot in common and were best friends for a long time. She had never hitchhiked before, but she joined me on my crazy pursuit of traveling on the cheap. Somehow, God was with us and kept us mostly unscathed in our travels. I'm not sure how I dared to do half the things I did back then; I would never do that now!

Mindy and I rented a room in a house in Brisbane. Michael was the owner of the house as well as our second roommate. We lived there for at least three months and worked at the World Expo Pavilion in Brisbane in 1988.

One day, I made a call to my mum. It had been over a year since I had talked to her. Surprisingly, she answered the phone and actually wanted to talk to me. She seemed overjoyed that I had called.

"Hi, Davinder. It's really nice to hear from you. We have missed you. How long have you been in Australia?"

"About six months. I love it here, but I miss England. How is everyone? How are Dad, Mandeep, Kuljeet and Sabina?" I missed them all and was so happy to be speaking to my mum again.

"Everyone is doing well. Come home. We will forget everything that happened; we just need you to come home."

The sincerity in my mother's voice convinced me she truly wanted me back home, so I relented. I must have been ready to go home, and I had missed them all, as well as England. Australia was a beautiful country, but it was so remote and so far away. Sometimes, I had been very homesick.

"Mum, I'll look into getting a ticket and let you know once I've booked it," I promised.

"Sounds good, Davinder. Take care, and we will talk to you soon. Bye."

"Bye, Mum."

We ended the call, and I immediately began looking into flights to England.

I went home while Mindy went off to Canberra to meet up with a boy she had met in Brisbane.

I stopped by Copenhagen first. I wanted to visit Peter and pick up some of my belongings. I wouldn't be moving back with him; I had realized this while in Australia. It was apparent to both of us that we had grown apart.

I spent a few hours in Peter's apartment. He promised to mail my Indian jewelry, but unfortunately, I never received anything. I'm not sure if this is because Peter was a little bitter with me, or if they really got lost in the mail as he'd stated on a phone call when I asked about the items. I had arrived in Copenhagen on a Sunday. If I had wanted to retrieve the items myself, I would have had to change my flight so I could get to the bank on Monday. I didn't want to do that. Still, it was good that I got the opportunity to see Peter in person after so much time away from him.

My family threw a party for me when I returned to Hull in 1989. I quickly realized things hadn't changed. Even though I was twenty years old, my freedom was restricted. I couldn't go out in the evening or hang out with my friends, and I was expected to help with the shop and the housework.

It wasn't long before I left home once again and went to London. After two months in London, I purchased another one-way ticket to Australia. I went with my friend Judith this time. We arrived with very little money, probably less than a $100 each, so we had to get jobs very quickly. Judith and I hitchhiked from Sydney to Brisbane and then to Melbourne. This second stay involved more time in Melbourne, and I ended up being in Australia for another six months. Eventually, I returned to England for about two years while Judith stayed on in Melbourne. Initially, I'd gone back to Hull, but I couldn't stay home for too long and ended up going back to London after about two months.

I spent over a year working at a hotel in Bayswater, near Paddington. I also did various other odd jobs until I decided to fly out to New York City, a place I had visited on my way back from Australia. I was surprised at how much I liked it. I had never wanted to visit the United States because I'd always been more fascinated with Australia. My trip to New York is the reason I'm in the States today.

Hello, America

After a brief stay in New York, I lived on the East Coast in Washington, DC. Since I've been in America, I've had several relationships. I met and married a wonderful man in Washington, DC, but unfortunately, that relationship lasted a year. I got married a third time—this time in Maryland—to my oldest daughter's father. I was with him for less than a year. I guess marriage and I don't mix well!

Seven years later, I moved to San Diego after falling in love with the city on a prior trip. I met my two youngest children's father here in San Diego; however, I did not marry him, but the relationship lasted ten years! We started to grow apart during the last three years of the relationship, until we finally went our own ways when our youngest daughter was only seven months old. I devoted myself to raising my three kids as a single parent and working full time.

I finally realized I have to focus on myself and my happiness again, and I was determined to try online dating to meet someone. In fact, it became a New Year's resolution of mine in 2018 that by the time I reached my fiftieth birthday in October of that year, I would try online dating because San Diego isn't an easy place to meet someone. I'm not sure why. I hadn't been looking, but no one came my way either. If I left it that way, I could have reached a hundred years of age and remained single and lonely, and I was determined not to let that happen. However, I let that entire year go and turned fifty, still alone and single.

In September of 2019, I discovered a speed dating organization and paid a small fee to sit with several men and try to learn as much about them as possible in just five minutes. I won't talk too much about that, but it resulted in matching with someone. I went on two dates with him, but there was no chemistry.

I finally tried online dating in September of 2020, the year of the pandemic and not the best time to meet a potential partner. I went on a few dates with about three different men, until I finally met the fourth man in January of 2021. I'm happy to say I'm still with him at the time I'm writing this book (it's currently September of 2021).

I still strongly believe in romance, and I'd like to think he's my Prince Charming. He's a wonderful guy, and we have a lot in common. I still haven't ruled out marriage, even though I feel bad that I've been married three times.

Family Dynamics and My Life Now

Now that I've settled here in America, I've created new habits and enjoyed different experiences. I stay away from ironing as much as I can. I find it alleviates the need to spend countless hours ironing if I take the clothes straight from the dryer and hang them up or fold them and put them away. I've reclaimed hours of my life in other little ways such as finding uncooked tortillas at the grocery store that taste just like homemade *rotis* once cooked. Now I don't have to spend all that time and energy making the dough for *chapattis* and rolling them out. Any time saved in this busy day and age is a bonus to me. I don't order my children around or try to control them. I still have to watch myself because I'm guilty of controlling and micro-managing to some degree, but my children let me know so I can take a step back and think about it.

I'm the opposite of my mother in some regards. Where she controlled us with household chores, I haven't done the same with my children. For years, I did all the dishes. They didn't want to participate, and I didn't want to force them. I went to the other extreme of giving them the freedom to be children. Eventually, I found there must be a balance. It's good if children help—one person shouldn't do it all alone—but there should never be force or control, only understanding and cooperation from the individuals themselves. I'm happy to report that just as recently as 2019, both of my youngest children help with the dishes, and we take turns. They realized I needed help, and this is the best way for us to work together.

How is my relationship with my family today? I'm sad to say my mother isn't talking to me for the second time in my life. Her disownment of me still has to do with my forced marriage. After I left my husband, nearly two years passed before she accepted me again. We have visited one another from time to time, even though I live in the United States and she lives in England. She and the rest of my family came to San Diego for the first time in 2001, following the birth of my second child. It was a great visit and wonderful for my oldest daughter, who was only four years old at the time.

My family and I have made numerous visits to England. We spend about four days in London before heading north to visit family in Hull. We've taken family vacations together, including a cruise in 2006 and a trip to Turkey in 2014. However, when I started speaking out about my forced marriage story in 2019, my mum found out and stopped talking to me. Starting in September 2019, I have had no communication with her, including no birthday calls or texts. Just knowing that the problem she created—my forced marriage—has resulted in her not speaking to me twice in my lifetime is too much for me to fathom.

What I experienced years ago haunts me to this day. My mum would prefer for me to stay quiet and for the whole world not to know what happened to me. Her family honor has come into question, and she feels attacked, but that's never been my goal. My only goal is to raise awareness by telling my story in its entirety. I know many girls and women out there can relate to my experience. My situation wasn't an isolated incident; unfortunately, it happens to thousands of women and girls every day.

Many people think I should be able to speak to my mum about my feelings. In 2006, she slapped me across the face when I told her she never should have arranged my marriage to Bik. She was so angry that I even had the nerve to speak those words to her. She refuses to participate in these conversations with any one of us. If she feels it becomes too personal or we're questioning her, she will put us in our place, just like she did when we were children. On the final night of our last visit to England just after New Year's Day in 2018, my brother told my mum she had done a lot of damage.

"You spoilt our lives and don't really care what you did to us. You controlled us in everything you did, not caring about our feelings or thoughts. You arranged all our marriages and just rushed to get it done. You tossed our dad out of the house, not caring where he went. You've pushed her away to the other side of the world and we hardly ever get to see her," he said, pointing at me.

"How dare you accuse me!" my mum yelled. "How dare you speak to me like that? You have no respect after everything I've done for you. How can you even stand in front of me and have the nerve to talk to me like that? I think it's best that you leave from this house. We don't need you here. You haven't been doing anything other than just coming here to get your food made and clothes washed. You treat your wife like a slave, and never once have you shown her any consideration or spent any quality time with her. How dare you!"

The yelling continued; it was truly horrible. It certainly wasn't the way I wanted to spend our last evening at home. The atmosphere was fraught with tension, pent-up feelings, and frustrations and traumas that had been buried for a very long time. It was really sad.

I felt bad for my brother. I like my sister-in-law, but my brother didn't deserve what happened to him, just like we didn't deserve what happened to us. He'd had a few drinks that night, but I guess that's what it takes for some people to say what's on their minds. It's very difficult for boys from my culture to open up. I think boys from *any* culture might have the same inability or reluctance to open up. Boys are expected to be tougher and not dwell on failures. They can go years, if not their whole entire lives, not speaking about the abuses they've suffered, whereas girls will open up much more freely or easily. This has got to stop; it must be taking a toll on boys if they feel they are not allowed to speak about such things just because they are boys. It's not fair. We certainly don't want them suffering from mental health issues, and I care greatly about my brother and his life too.

In some ways, I'm happy to be far away from England and my family because these dramas could fill entire episodes on a television show. Our family is a drama of its own. I do miss England though. I miss my family, my friends, the television programs, the food, and so much more, but more than being away from England, I must be away from my family in order to heal.

Most of all, I have to be away from my mother because she won't admit what she's done wrong. I don't entirely blame her. She did her best to carry on traditions, but when we begged her to listen to us, she didn't care enough to acknowledge our pain or help us through the healing process. We need her to be part of the conversation and be strong enough to admit she made mistakes, even if she didn't do anything intentionally. That would be an amazing start.

Life is too short and too precious, and I want to have a relationship with my mother again. I see her importance in my life; I wouldn't be here without her, and nobody can replace my mother. Treasure your mother and love her beyond everything. I've tried to do this; in fact, I *have* done this. I love my mother to this very day, but I feel she has never cared or wanted to reciprocate that love, no matter what I do.

Mum never came to help me during any of my three pregnancies. Many women have mothers who live in other countries, but they manage to travel to their daughters during their pregnancies or right after they've given birth. My mother has stayed with me several times, even once right after my youngest was born, but it wasn't to help with the baby. She didn't do grandmotherly things, like looking after the baby or changing diapers. She only wanted to go shopping.

One afternoon, I approached her in a very hesitant manner.

"Mum, I need to be able to spend more time with the baby. When I go shopping with you all, I often miss her feeding time or forget to change her diaper as quickly as I normally would. I would prefer to stay home and tend to the baby properly."

"You don't know how to organize your time properly so you can do other things. You spend way too much time *wasting* time, being slow with everything."

I had always been the brunt of her criticism, even when she stayed with me. She's never seemed happy and has always been ready to attack and show her displeasure.

Part of me realizes I've had enough of this toxic behavior. If she wants to be this way and doesn't truly care for me for whatever reason, I am best not making further efforts to try to get her back into my life. I've tried though. I've called several times, but she has ignored me. I think she might have blocked me; my messages don't go through anymore.

Because of all of this, I am determined to build my happiness here with my kids, and hopefully, I will remarry one day. It would be great if I could have my family in my life, but I will have to learn to have to deal with it if they don't want to be a part of my future. I will always love my mother and want a relationship with her, but I need to do what is best for *my* well-being. I've resolved to going about my life until she realizes she was wrong.

I never talked to my dad about that horrible night in Denmark. He never apologized for not doing the right thing for me either. I don't know if he felt sorry for it or if he truly believed I was in the wrong. My father passed away in 2008, right before my youngest daughter was born, and I took his death very personally. Regardless of everything we'd been through, he was my dad. He was on holiday in India and was due to go back to England the day after he passed away. Unfortunately, he never made it out of his hotel room. I think the thought of him being alone traumatized me more than his death did.

Telling My Story for The First Time

I had already completed many college credits by the time I began studying at San Diego State University. This is where I earned my bachelor's degree in business administration. I was adamant to get the education I had been denied after high school. It was difficult trying to fit college into my schedule with a full-time job. It made me realize all these kids who were younger than me were doing it the way it should be done. It's best to go to college right after high school, just like I'd wanted to.

A professor once asked my class why we were in college at that juncture in our lives and what we wanted to study. The kids before me stood up and said they wanted to be a lawyer, teacher, and so forth, and they were intent on finishing their degree to the best of their ability to get where they wanted to be.

When it was my turn, I answered the question. Since I was an older student, I had more to say, and my own answer surprised even myself when I saw the reaction on the other students' faces as well as the reaction of my professor.

"I am studying for my bachelor's degree in business administration with an emphasis in management. I have had experience running my own restaurant, but I've always wanted a degree. The reason I'm in college at age thirty-nine, almost forty, is because I wasn't allowed to go to college right after high school. My parents had other plans for me. I wasn't allowed to go to college because I was supposed to get married instead. A marriage had been arranged for me from the age of fourteen."

I could sense the shock and amazement in the room, and I realized what I'd said wasn't normal for the rest of the world. This was so hugely different and bizarre that I suddenly shocked myself with my own truth. I'd always thought what had happened to me was normal, but I finally understood it wasn't. Something awoke in me that day—the spirit of a revelation, the truth of what had happened to me, and the first time I had really given my situation any serious thought since my arranged marriage occurred when I was eighteen.

I hadn't given it much thought after I left my husband in Denmark all those years ago. Finally, at thirty-nine years old, I began to think about what had transpired in my life. I hadn't expected any questions that probed into my past or present, but when I think back on it now, the professor's question was valid and wouldn't be that unusual or difficult to answer for most people. Of course, my answer was loaded with a shocking response. I hadn't meant for it to be shocking, but it was the reality of my situation and I had blurted out the truth. I now had to prepare for the next class; we had been assigned to make a presentation on what we had just talked about. My professor stopped me on my way out of the room.

"Davinder, it's important for the class to hear about your culture and how it isn't always a given that everyone can go to college, for whatever reasons. Do you mind expanding on the cultural expectations of your family and giving us more details about your arranged marriage, or however much you can tell us?"

"Of course, I can do that."

I was a trembling mess. I had a natural fear of speaking in front of a crowd of people; I was shy, to say the least. In high school, I froze when it was my turn to talk in front of the class. My head grew warm, and I thought I was going to pass out. How was I going to do this?

I prepared by writing an outline. I worried about saying too much because I didn't think that was what my teacher was looking for. I was able to find an excerpt from what I had written for the class when I was thirty-nine:

> *When I was fourteen, I was engaged to be married in an arranged wedding, which occurred when I was eighteen. My parents considered marriage more important than education. I did not want to get married and had stronger feelings about it as the big event drew closer. The marriage, which took place in Denmark to an Indian immigrant, ended up in a quick divorce, as I knew immediately the man that I married was not for me. My parents were heartbroken and mad at me. I then stayed and worked in Denmark for a year.*

This is what I read aloud at the next class meeting. It wasn't as hard as I thought it would be. My classmates were in shock, and many told me afterward that they were grateful I had shared my story with them. That was a new experience for me, one that left me wondering about this new revelation of speaking up about what I'd experienced.

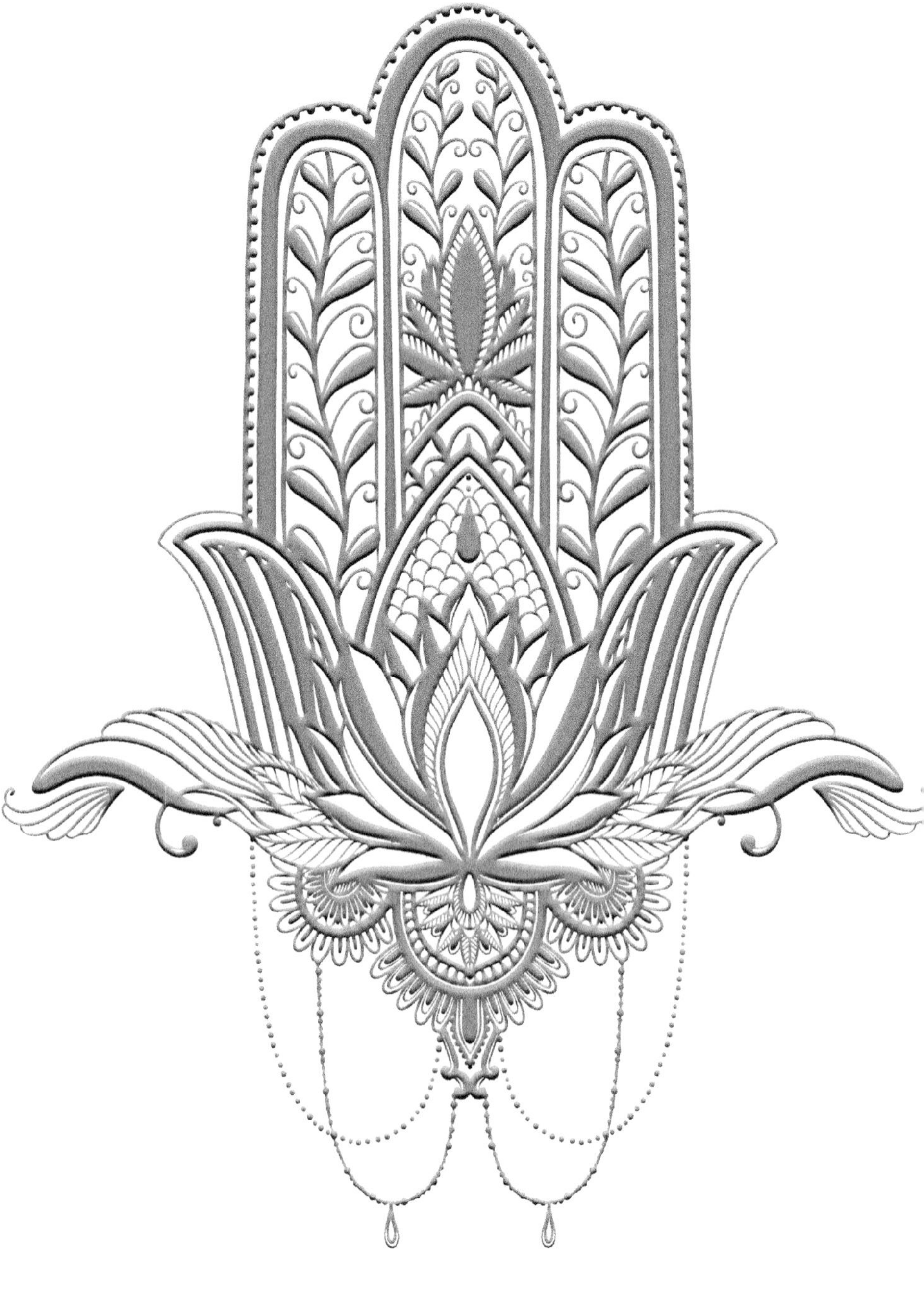

Discovering Others Like Me and My Path to Activism

Shortly after I graduated the following year, I delved into the world of social media. I had begun working from home as a home-based travel agent, and to promote my travel business, I joined Twitter in 2011. I initially planned to only tweet about travel, but I stumbled across arranged and forced marriage articles, as well as child marriage stories, and I was mesmerized. These stories were so familiar; it was almost like I was reading my own.

I came across Jasvinder Sanghera[2], the founder of the United Kingdom charity Karma Nirvana[3] for forced marriage survivors. She started Karma Nirvana in honor of her sister, Robina, who was deeply unhappy in her forced marriage and subsequently died by suicide.

---

2   Jasvinder Sanghera https://www.jasvindersanghera.com/
3   Karma Nirvana https://karmanirvana.org.uk/

My heart broke when I read her story. Her pain was my pain, and it was almost like we were the same person. We had nearly identical stories of being forced into marriage based off a picture we were shown at the age of fourteen. Jasvinder ran away at sixteen and stayed away. She turned out to be a strong individual who, based on her own inner beliefs, saw the need early on to be different. I relate so much to her determination to create her own path.

Jasvinder is my hero. She not only ran away from a forced marriage, but she stayed away and created something to help others avoid the pain her sister and so many other survivors experience. I can't begin to explain how much it means to people like me to have an organization that helps these vulnerable children. It is an amazing and much-needed service. Now, other forced marriage survivors have a place they can turn to for help.

There was no organization like this when I was growing up in England and now there are at least thirty or forty charities involved in assisting victims of forced marriage and honor-based abuse. Jasvinder was the trailblazer who started this line of help for victims, and others followed her lead. She is a remarkable woman, and I'm so proud to have met her when she came to San Diego. She, along with Paula Kweskin, producer of *Honor Diaries*[4], and Raheel Raza with the Council for Muslims Facing Tomorrow[5], were being honored for their part in tirelessly working on behalf of women's human rights. That was a wonderful and special evening for me. The reception held on their behalf was in a home in Rancho Santa Fe, and I was personally invited by Jasvinder.

Right now, I know of three organizations that are trying to help victims of child marriage here in the United States: Unchained

---

4   Honor Diaries https://www.imdb.com/title/tt3135012/
5   Council for Muslims Facing Tomorrow https://muslimsfacingtomorrow.com/

At Last[6], Tahirih Justice Center[7], and the AHA Foundation[8]. I sometimes feel the United States is about twenty steps behind the United Kingdom in fighting human rights abuses, but I'm so grateful these organizations exist and awareness is beginning to happen here. Currently, I am trying to put an end to child marriage in California, where girls can still be forced into marriage before the age of eighteen. To add to that, I want to criminalize it and help with any existing efforts. I believe we can all be part of change, and we all must work together to combat these harmful practices that hold girls prisoner and deprive us of our human rights.

In February of 2020, I went to Assembly Member Brian Maienschein's office in San Diego and met with his staff member, Rob Knudsen. I presented my petition, which had only 216 signatures at that time, and I shared my story. Rob graciously listened to me and seemed to be very moved and willing to help. He mentioned I should get organizations behind me; this would be the way to move forward. He wanted to know if anyone had ever introduced that type of legislation in California, and I didn't know the answer. During my research, I discovered Sara Tasneem, whom I would later share a platform with, had spoken in front of Congress with hopes of ending child marriage with her testimony when SB 273 was presented as the possible bill that could have ended child marriages in California.

While Senate Bill 273 was introduced by Senator Jerry Hill in September of 2018 and became effective in January 2019, it wasn't the bill we'd hoped for. It stated, "no marriages for anyone under the age of eighteen were allowed without exception." Instead, legislators introduced clauses that didn't fully help the cause. Currently, judges sign off on marriages if they see parental consent on a marriage petition. How do judges not know that parental

---

6   Unchained At Last https://www.unchainedatlast.org/
7   Tahirih Justice Center https://www.tahirih.org/
8   AHA Foundation https://www.theahafoundation.org/

consent isn't what they should be looking at? In fact, they should be questioning it. When are they going to learn it is often the parents who are coercing the children into these marriages? By judges not being well-informed, their signature on these agreements makes them complicit in child abuse.

None of us can rest until child marriage is a tradition of the past, not just here in California, but in every state in the United States of America and every country around the world.

My meeting with the staff member was an integral part to my taking concrete steps to move forward and be part of the change that is needed. By bringing this to their attention, I had started a conversation. I then listened to the staff member's suggestions and contacted Unchained At Last. Since then, I have become a volunteer for Unchained At Last and signed up as a mentor. Hopefully, I will be able to start mentoring other forced marriage victims who may need my help and insight. I am also part of their initiative, The National Coalition to End Child Marriage[9] in the United States. This grassroots effort to spread awareness was started by Unchained At Last and Equality Now. Unchained At Last introduced me to Global Hope 365[10], and I signed on to their California Coalition to End Child Marriage[11]. I now hope that, with the help of the California Coalition to End Child Marriage and Unchained At Last, a new bill will soon be introduced in California with no exceptions under the age of eighteen for child marriage. Currently, the marriage age has been raised to eighteen in only six states: New Jersey, Delaware, Minnesota, Pennsylvania, Rhode Island, and New York. A link where up to date statistics can be obtained on

---

9   The National Coalition to End Child Marriage https://endchildmarriageus.org/
10 Global Hope 365 https://www.globalhope365.org/
11 California Coalition to End Child Marriage https://cacoalitiontoendchildmarriage.org/2019/09/14/global-hope-365-launches-california-coalition-to-end-child-marriage/

child marriage in the USA is available here[12].

It's also important to note that the U.S. Department of State views forced marriage as a human rights abuse[13], and in the case of minors, a form of child abuse. The European Parliament has labeled forced marriage a "violation of human rights and a form of gender-based violence." Denmark, Germany, Spain, Belgium, Slovakia, and the United Kingdom have criminalized the practice.

Below is an excerpt of the U.S. Government's view of forced marriage (taken from https://www.uscis.gov/humanitarian/forced-marriage):

> *"The U.S. government is opposed to forced marriage and considers it to be a serious human rights abuse. If the victim of forced marriage is a child, forced marriage is also a form of child abuse.*
>
> *The U.S. government is working in the United States and abroad to end the practice and to assist individuals who have been forced into marriage or are at risk of being forced into marriage.*
>
> *In some U.S. states, forced marriage is a crime, and in all U.S. states, people who force someone to marry may be charged with violating state laws, including those against domestic violence, child abuse, rape, assault, kidnapping, threats of violence, stalking, or coercion. People who force someone to marry may also face significant immigration consequences, such as being inadmissible to or removable from the United States."*

---

12   https://www.unchainedatlast.org/laws-to-end-child-marriage/
13   https://www.uscis.gov/humanitarian/forced-marriage

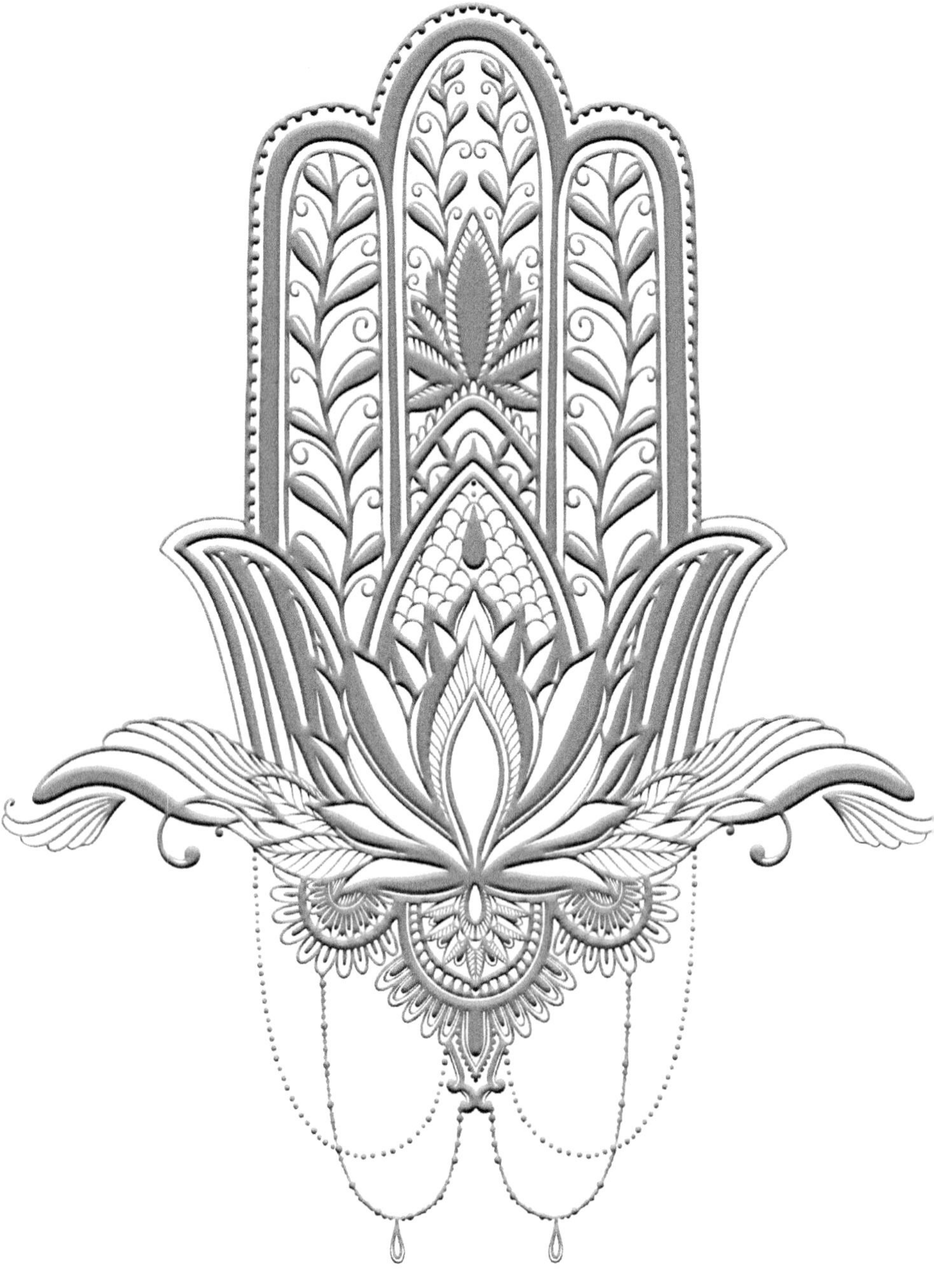

Why Forced Marriages and Child Marriages Have to be Illegal

As mentioned previously, honor killings are harmful practices that we all must put an end to. Nobody deserves to be murdered by their own family just because they stood up for themselves and said "no" to an arranged wedding or child marriage. Honor killings continue to happen all over the world, and I'm surprised there are so many people who don't even know what these are.

Here in America, we just recently are on our way toward getting justice for Sarah and Amina Said, two sisters from Dallas, Texas, who were murdered by their father, Yaser Said, in 2008. He was on the run for many years after shooting them in the back of his taxi. He was on America's Top Ten Most Wanted Fugitives list for years but evaded capture. His family shielded and protected him all those years. He finally was caught on August 26, 2020. I was incredibly overjoyed that day. I know I was joined in my excitement by many others who rejoiced in the fact these two beautiful girls would finally get the justice they deserved. The girls were killed because they simply wanted freedom and were considered too Westernized. They didn't want the arranged marriages their father was trying to force on them. He hated that they had boyfriends.

They were not to blame, as they were born and raised here. He should have expected this. Instead, this is another example of how culture gets in the way of freedom for those of us who have deep-rooted ancestral ties with other countries.

It's important for people not to think that these killings are just murders, and it's important to distinguish they are honor killings. Everyone needs to know families from certain cultures care more about what the community thinks than they care about their own kids. They will retaliate by taking the life of their child to save their reputation within the community. It's important to spread awareness so that those who are voiceless and have died from honor killings don't continue to be a number. They need to be remembered and receive justice so this never happens again.

Sarah and Amina Said, Banaz Mahmod, Jasvinder Sidhu from Canada, Noor Alameki from Arizona, Shafilea Ahmed from the UK, and so many other girls and boys deserve better. Their parents didn't care about them and won't honor their memories.

Each year on July 14th, Karma Nirvana holds a Day of Remembrance, also known as Day of Memory, where these victims are honored by those who mourn their loss and the tragedy that surrounded their short lives. They stood up for themselves and had the strength to attempt to carve their own destiny. For this, they paid a horrible price, but we cannot let fear intimidate us, and we must spread awareness. Until we make forced marriage and child marriage illegal, parents won't change their mind frames and break the traditions of the past. If we don't make forced marriage and child marriage illegal everywhere in the world, girls and boys will continue to be murdered in these ruthless honor killings, and we cannot let this practice continue.

Subsequent Speaking Events

Since I began writing this book, I have participated in ten speaking events. My first was in 2019 with Ahaana, a local non-profit in San Diego. Ahaana[14] strives to promote awareness of the South Asian culture. I will always be extremely grateful to Nanda Mehta for giving me my first opportunity to tell my story in public. I was able to practice in front of her and the team who would all tell their stories alongside me. This was a necessary first step for me as I prepared to step out of my comfort zone and delve into the world of public speaking.

Nanda's annual show, *Yoni Ki Baat*, is a collaborative of people telling their personal stories and is inspired by Eve Ensler's *The Vagina Monologues*. I told my forced marriage tale to approximately 190 people in the audience. It was a beautiful day, and the venue was amazing. The University of San Diego is a breathtaking campus. I had a great time bonding with my fellow presenters in

---

14   Ahaana https://www.ahaana.org/

the dressing room before the event. The other performers had their own narratives on subjects as diverse as special needs, parenting, adoption, abuse, neglect, and widowhood. Each account was extremely powerful. It was an incredible event.

My last public speaking event in 2020 was really special for me. I arranged and organized United Against Harmful Practices with the help of two volunteers from MiraCosta College, a local college in San Diego. It was there that I earned my associates in arts degree in business administration in 2008. The volunteers assisted me with the Zoom link, processed the EventBrite registrations, and administrated the inner workings of the Zoom meeting when we went live. I'm proud to say Jasvinder Sanghera, the founder of Karma Nirvana, was in attendance and graciously offered to moderate the event.

The program lineup included Fraidy Reiss, the founder of Unchained At Last, the only organization dedicated to ending child and forced marriage in the United States of America. Fraidy is a survivor of a forced marriage that happened when she was nineteen. Payzee Mahmod, Sara Tasneem, and Dawn Tyree completed the list. Sara and Dawn are also child marriage survivors whose marriages occurred in the United States. Payzee is a child marriage survivor who lives in the United Kingdom and whose sister, Banaz, was murdered by her family for leaving her marriage. Banaz's murder was an honor killing.

Payzee is a strong, courageous woman, activist, and advocate for women's and girls' rights, as are all the women who were on the panel for United Against Harmful Practices. It's great that Payzee continues to be the voice reminding everyone about the plight that befell her sister. Payzee is currently spearheading a huge movement in the United Kingdom to end child marriage and make it illegal. I sincerely hope it will happen. I think it's easier to pass legislation like that in a place like the United Kingdom. In the United States, each state passes its own legislation, and it's frustrating that it can't be made illegal all over the country at the same time. Criminalization of forced marriage took effect in June 2014 in England and Wales and in October 2014 in Scotland. Forced marriage is a crime in some of the United States, but it's not criminal everywhere, and it really needs to be.

    I felt incredibly fortunate to have these great women agree to be a part of United Against Harmful Practices. I was privileged and honored to share the platform with them. The conference was held virtually due to the Coronavirus Pandemic that plagued not only our nation but the entire world. It would have been wonderful to have been under the same roof with these amazing women! United Against Harmful Practices - Zoom Meeting on Child Marriage/Forced Marriage - June 13th, 2020[15] is on YouTube. It can be used as an educational tool that can ultimately help increase awareness that this plight is very real and is happening throughout the world. If survivors speak out and share their very real stories, only then will people understand the true horrors of what happens in the world. Hopefully, the testimonies of others will encourage people to band together and take a stance against this injustice.

---

15   United Against Harmful Practices - Zoom Meeting on Child Marriage/Forced Marriage - June 13th, 2020 https://www.youtube.com/watch?v=sc-adj6GLYc&t=3449s

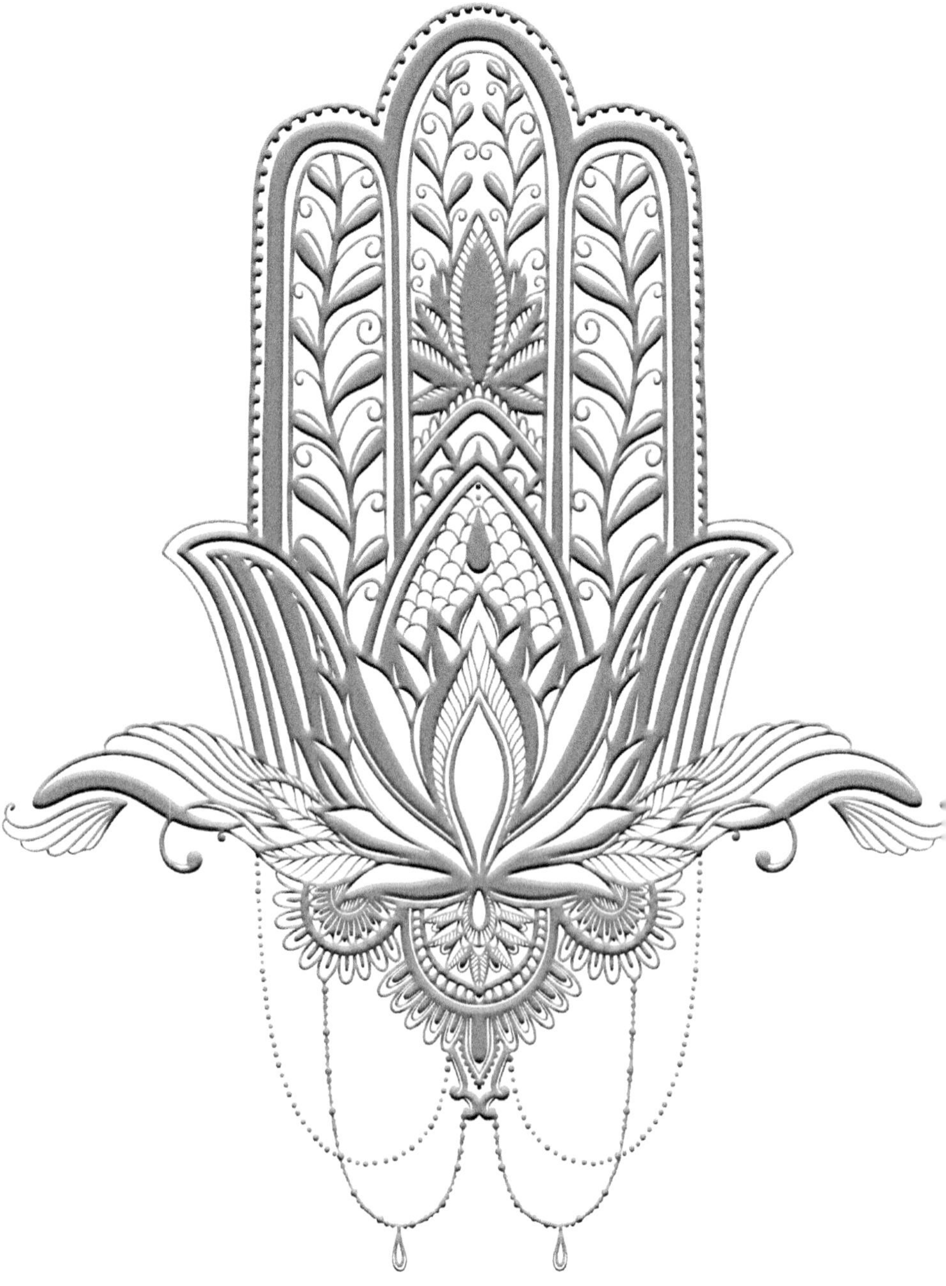

Conclusion

If we don't speak up and tell the world about the atrocities that were inflicted on us, how will the world learn and be able to take steps in the right direction so this doesn't happen to any other person?

This disgusting practice of forced and child marriage is in every country all over the world. Every day, hundreds, if not thousands, of people are complicit in human rights abuses: the judge who signs off on court orders, the priest who officiates the ceremony of a minor with an adult, the parents who allow this to happen, the baker who makes a business of profiting off the demise of a young child, the villagers who feast on food at a party that celebrates the marriage.

What about the teachers who stayed quiet and didn't help us when they were the ones who could have made a difference in our lives if they had just tried to talk to us and educate us about our rights? Why don't they try to question the sense of it, especially whether it makes sense for a fifteen-year-old to be married? It's an insult to us when these adults stay quiet and choose not to interfere in our lives because they don't want to risk being called racist or accused of interfering with our culture.

Many ignorant parents will call allies "racists" to stop them from stepping in. These parents use the color of their skin as a defense for their actions. Their logic is, "We are different because of this, and others shouldn't interfere with us because of our difference." Ideologies like this are intrinsically entwined in our culture and traditions. However, no one has the right to abuse, and no one should force marriage upon anyone. We really need to stop hiding behind culture and traditions and using these as excuses for continuing traditions that inflict this very abuse upon innocent victims.

We need to stand up to those who use claims of racism to hide behind their wrongs and scare off those who *want* to help but don't because they fear being attacked. Not only are the parents wrong to use the racism card or hide behind culture and tradition, but the teachers, the police, and those in positions of authority are also wrong for not being brave enough to stand up for us.

If you know something isn't right, have the guts to stand up to it, no matter if you will be attacked for it. It is not racist to care about human rights; it's not racist to have a heart. It's actually very cruel and unfeeling of those in a position to help who choose not to do so. It is cowardly to be scared about having your character attacked versus caring about children and their safety. I believe there is a lot of work that still needs to be done.

Education has to happen at the schools and colleges where teachers are on the frontline to educate their students about human rights. They need to know they have the right not to be forced into marriage, and they have the right to marry who they want, when they want. When parents cannot be trusted to always have the best interests of their kids at heart, then why should these kids be left to rely upon the guidance of their parents, especially if they are steered into forced marriage due to culture and tradition? We are not caring enough about our children if we're not doing everything to protect their best interests.

These lessons and information should be available to kids so they can have a more broadened horizon of facts. We have to do this for our children so no one else is victimized the way so many of us have been. Survivors can only do so much in sharing their stories on social media or at events. The rest has to be done through education. Educating the young is the way forward. Most parents refuse to listen to the new way of thinking and wish to hang on to their belief systems of tradition and culture, but we have to let it be known that some traditions are best broken because they don't work and have no place in today's society.

How can child marriage be viable when it places girls at such a disadvantage? They lose the rights to a future, to freedom, to education, to financial independence, and even to literacy. The circle of abuse will be perpetuated where girls are never allowed to be free, as they will remain in a cycle of poverty due to being robbed of their full potential. Education is their way to a better life, a chance of getting a good job, and the opportunity to rise above where they started.

The potential for pregnancy in a forced marriage is high. Kids' bodies aren't mature enough to handle childbirth, which puts the young mother and the baby at risk of suffering a multitude of complications. Their babies might be born premature and could be placed at a disadvantage of not even living to their first birthday. Or it could be a stillbirth. This is all so tragic and traumatic to the young mother who never asked for this.

Is it fair for a girl to be married to a stranger and placed in danger? Her physical and mental well-being are at risk from the moment the arrangement is made. This sounds wrong to me, and I hope it sounds wrong to everybody who thinks about this abominable situation.

I'm astonished child marriage is allowed to continue. Child marriages are happening in countries such as the United States and the United Kingdom. This is unacceptable and unbelievable and it *must* change. Child marriage may have been appropriate hundreds of years ago—it never should have been okay—but it should *not* be happening now or ever again. Victims have spoken up; voices have been heard. No one should be drowning out these very real stories of pain and suffering. These women and girls need to be listened to and something must be done about this plight. Let's all join together to end forced marriage and child marriage.

How to Find Out More

Now I have a voice! Yes, my voice was suppressed when I was younger, and I continued to let it be suppressed because I was not totally free. I have freed myself and have the voice that is desperately needed. I use it for my fellow sisters, those who may still be fighting the struggle right now and those who are still locked up in forced marriages and child marriages and don't have the strength to get away. I need to use it for those who might find themselves in my very same situation but hopefully will get help before it gets that far. I never want anyone to have to go through what I and hundreds of thousands of other girls have gone through. No one's human rights should be violated.

You can find me on the following platforms:

Twitter @luchanik
https://twitter.com/luchanik

@angel4many
https://twitter.com/angel4many

Facebook @luchanik
https://www.facebook.com/luchanik

Wordpress @luchanik
https://luchanik.com/about/

Pinterest @luchanik
https://www.pinterest.com/Luchanik/

Instagram @luchanik
https://www.instagram.com/luchanik/

Youtube @luchanik
https://www.youtube.com/user/luchaniktravel

I also now have a petition[16] on Change.org and would love for everyone to sign and share it so that others can sign it too.

I will continue to speak up as much as I can and whenever I get the opportunity. I intend to contribute to change for the better. My hope is to be part of the change needed so forced marriage and child marriage around the world will become a thing of the past.

---

16   https://www.change.org/EndChildMarriageAndEndForcedMarriage

About the Author

Davinder Kaur was born and raised in Bradford, England. She briefly lived in Denmark and traveled Australia for a year before moving to the United States in the early 1990s. She earned her bachelor's degree at the age of forty while working full time and raising her three children who are her pride and joy.

She enjoys cooking and traveling, loves cruises, and her two favorite places thus far are Italy and London. You can find Davinder on Twitter or Instagram @luchanik or visit her website at https://luchanik.com.

Davinder is the survivor of a forced marriage. Forced to Marry Him: A Lifetime of Tradition and the Will to Break It is her first book.